The Art of GLUTEN-FREE HOMEMADE BREAD

Written by Rachel Parks and Carolyn Thomas for

Copyright © 2023 Homesteading Family
All rights reserved.

Dedication

To all those who miss good, nutritious bread.

Contents

1. The Challenge of Gluten-Free ... 1
2. How to Use this Book ... 3
3. What About Ancient Grains? ... 5
4. Gluten-Free Flours and Their Purpose ... 9
5. Baking Mixes and Flour Blends ... 17
6. Dough Binders and Enhancers ... 23
7. Gluten-Free Substitutions ... 27
8. Gluten-Free Baking Primer ... 49
9. Gluten-Free Sourdough ... 61
    Sourdough Starter Questions and Troubleshooting ... 70
10. Baked Goods Recipes ... 79
    Baking Blends ... 79
        All-Purpose Gluten-Free Flour Baking Blend ... 79
        Whole Grain Gluten-Free Baking Blend ... 80
    Pancakes and Waffles ... 81
        Pancakes ... 81
        Waffles ... 81
    Sourdough Pancakes and Waffles ... 82
        Sourdough Pancakes ... 82
        Sourdough Waffles ... 82
    Muffins ... 84
        Raspberry Lemon Muffins ... 85
        Blueberry Lemon Muffins ... 85
        Carrot Cake Muffins ... 85
        Double Chocolate Chip Muffins ... 85
        Blackberry Lime Muffins ... 86
        Blueberry Lemon Sourdough Muffins ... 87
        Banana Chocolate Chip Sourdough Muffins ... 88
        Carrot Cake Sourdough Muffins ... 89
        Savory Garlic Herb Sourdough Muffins ... 90
    Quick Breads ... 91
        Simple Quick Bread ... 91
        Easy Vanilla Icing ... 92

- Pumpkin Bread ... 93
- Gluten-Free Cookies ... 94
  - Chocolate Chip Cookies ... 95
  - Double Chocolate Chip Cookies ... 95
  - Lemon Drop Cookies ... 95
  - Peanut Butter Oatmeal Cookies ... 95
  - Oatmeal Raisin Cookies ... 95
- Biscuits & Scones ... 96
  - Biscuits ... 96
  - Chocolate Chip Scones ... 97
  - Cranberry Orange Scones ... 97
  - Lemon Raspberry Scones ... 97
  - Cinnamon Apple Scones ... 97
  - Banana Chocolate Chip Scones ... 98
  - Vanilla Cake ... 99
  - Vanilla Buttercream Frosting ... 99
  - Whipped Cream Frosting ... 100
  - Sourdough Vanilla Cake ... 101
  - Cake Brownies ... 102
  - Sourdough Brownies ... 103
  - Troubleshooting and Tips for Cakes & Brownies ... 104
- Doughnuts and Cinnamon Rolls ... 105
  - Cinnamon Rolls ... 105
  - Easy Vanilla Icing ... 106
  - Cake Doughnuts ... 108
  - Sourdough "Discard" Doughnuts: ... 110

11. Yeast Bread Recipes ... 113
- General Mixing, Baking, and Troubleshooting Tips for Yeast Breads ... 115
- Basic White Loaf Bread ... 118
- White Yeast Boule ... 121
- Troubleshooting Tips for Boules ... 123
- Basic Whole Grain Loaf Bread ... 124
- White Baguette or French Bread ... 127
- Buckwheat Boule ... 131
- Buns and Rolls ... 134

- Other Gluten-Free Breads ... 135
  - Pizza Crust ... 135
  - Flatbread ... 137
  - Herbed Focaccia ... 138

12. Sourdough Breads ... 143
- Troubleshooting Tips for Sourdough Breads ... 143
- Troubleshooting Tips for Sourdough Breads ... 144

White Sourdough Loaf 145
White Sourdough Boule 147
Troubleshooting Tips for Sourdough Boules 148
Whole Grain Sourdough Loaf 150
Whole Grain Sourdough Boule 153
Troubleshooting Tips for Sourdough Boules 154
Sourdough Buns and Rolls 156

13. Recommended Resources 157

Index 162

Acknowledgments

Thanks to all the grandmothers of yesterday and mothers of today who have taught the next generation how to bake from scratch.

To those who are facing new food allergies and sensitivities and are willing to brave the frontier of gluten-free baking:

...those who eat at your table thank you.

1. The Challenge of Gluten-Free

Gluten-free flours behave much differently than wheat-based flours. When you bake with a wheat-based flour, you add liquid to the dough and let it rest. Then, the proteins in the grain begin to form gluten structures which allow the dough to stretch. This is why wheat bread expands and rises during baking. Gluten-free flours don't stretch like gluten, so gluten-free baking relies on other methods to encourage reliable internal structures.

Glutenous grains like wheat, spelt, barley, and rye are unique because each kernel is a seed. If you soak one, it will sprout. Each kernel contains protein, starch, fat, vitamins, minerals, and enzymes: everything that a baby plant needs to grow. In contrast, many gluten-free flour blends are largely starch based (exceptions are amaranth, quinoa, buckwheat, millet, sorghum, teff, nut, and legume flours). Because gluten-free flours are mostly starch, you must use blends of several different gluten-free flours to mimic the nutritional profile and structure of glutenous grains. Using a single-source gluten-free flour (like brown rice, for example) will produce baked goods that are heavy, dense, and nutritionally unvaried.

This is the challenge that the gluten-free baker faces: coaxing starches, grains, and seeds into forms and combinations that are outside of their traditional uses in order to achieve an end product that tastes, looks, and feels like traditional breads and baked goods.

THE ART OF GLUTEN-FREE HOMEMADE BREAD

It can be daunting, but necessity and creativity beget invention. One Google search will show that there are thousands of recipes, blogs, and books devoted to gluten-free bread and baking. So why another?

The goal of this book is to give you a more intuitive sense of gluten-free baking. It is our hope that choosing flours, additives, and enhancers, and how these ingredients behave, will become less daunting. These recipes should be used as a starting point. Try them. Adjust them based on your palate and dietary needs. Tweak them and make them your own.

These recipes were written not only to maximize taste and texture, but also, and more importantly, nutrition. Many gluten-free recipes have an admirable goal of replicating the texture of gluten-full baked goods without the gluten. Unfortunately, this effect is best achieved using gluten-free flours that are heavily starch-based. As a contrast, this book aims to give you baked goods with a pleasant texture and comforting taste similar to gluten-based products without the cost of nourishing your body. You will see "white" bread recipes in this book, but the ingredients include nutrient-dense grains like sorghum, millet, and white bean flour. We believe your food should fill your belly, satisfy your soul, and nourish your body, all at the same time. We hope this book will help you do that.

Are you ready to take the gluten-free challenge? Then it's time to move on to Chapter 3 where we discuss ancient grains, what they are, and who should try them. After that, read through the chapters on gluten-free flours, baking mixes and their purpose, dough binders and enhancers, and a general primer on gluten-free baking. Our goal is to help you, the baker, learn the characteristics of each flour and determine which one is best suited for your purpose. In this way, you will learn how to successfully overcome the challenges of gluten-free baking. Happy baking everyone! Let's get going.

2. How to Use this Book

It seems pretty obvious how to use a recipe book, right? But The Art of Gluten-Free Bread is not your average recipe book. It is a class, an educational journey, and it is meant to be used as such, not just a collection of recipes with a touch of written story at the beginning.

As you are embarking on this journey you need to know right up front where you are heading. Your destination: intuitively baking gluten free breads and baked goods that are not 'good for gluten-free' but are just plain great, even if you are baking for people with very specific allergy profiles. You are going to learn how to make gluten free bread delicious and with a great texture, while still maintaining a high nutrient density. But you need to learn a few things along the way.

Read through the book in whatever order you like, but as you start to actually put what you learn into practice, come back to this roadmap to guide you on your learning journey.

STEP 1: Chapters 3, 4, 5, 6 and 7
Really get to know the ingredients involved in gluten-free baking. Learn what each type of flour does and how it can add to your baking. Learn about available gluten-free flour mixes, binders and more. Learn how to make substitutions in the case of the unavailability of an ingredient or in the case of intolerances to ingredients.

STEP 2: Chapter 8
Get to know the specifics of working with gluten-free flours and baking with a Gluten Free Baking Primer. You'll learn about the tips & tricks unique to gluten-free baking, and how to increase gluten-free digestibility.

STEP 3: Chapter 10
You aren't quite ready to make gluten-free breads, but it is time to start baking with your gluten-free flours. Make your own flour mix and whip up some wonderful goodies.

STEP 4: Chapter 9 and 10
It is time to jump into sourdough. Make your own starter and start using them in sourdough baked goods.

STEP 5: Chapter 11
Now dive into the yeast breads in the bread recipe section. You'll be amazed at how good these are.

STEP 6: Chapter 12
Now you are ready to dive into baking gluten free sourdough breads. Yay for the extra digestibility and nutrition!

STEP 7: You are now a Gluten-Free Master and can start serving others amazing, nutrient dense gluten free breads. Make sure you teach someone else in your life how to make their own amazing gluten-free goodies.

3. What About Ancient Grains?

What About Ancient Grains Like Spelt, Kamut, Einkorn, And Rye?

The seed structure of ancient grains like spelt, Khorasan (Kamut), einkorn, and rye is different from what we find in modern wheat. These ancient grains contain a different ratio of starch/protein/vitamins/minerals than their modern counterparts. Modern wheat is bred to have a larger kernel that is higher in starch. Some experts believe that people have difficulty digesting modern grains because the grain structure is no longer balanced properly. Many people who cannot tolerate modern wheat find that they can eat ancient grains like spelt, kamut, einkorn, or rye without any digestive issues. If you do NOT have celiac disease or a wheat allergy, it might be worth testing out these grains to see if you can tolerate them.

Einkorn: This ancient grain contains less starch and possesses a weaker gluten structure than modern wheat. It can be used measure-for-measure in place of whole wheat flour but absorbs moisture more slowly than regular wheat. It benefits from longer rest times to allow it more time to absorb all the liquid. Einkorn performs best with gentle folds or no-knead methods rather than kneading due to its weaker gluten structure. For this reason, avoid stand mixers for einkorn recipes as they can easily over-knead the dough. Hand-mixing is preferable. Additionally, set timers to prevent over-proofing as einkorn is not forgiving if over-risen. Bake when 30-50% proofed compared to regular wheat breads. Due to the lower starch content, the texture of einkorn benefits from recipes that include eggs, but good lean bread can be made with einkorn without using an enriched dough.

Khorasan (Kamut) Flour: This is an earthy, golden, ancient variety of wheat very similar in texture and performance to whole wheat pastry flour. This grain contains gluten, but many people who cannot tolerate wheat find that they can eat Khorasan without trouble. Though it can be substituted measure-for-measure in most recipes that call for wheat, Khorasan has a more delicate gluten structure than regular wheat and benefits from increased rest time and gentle kneading techniques.

Spelt Flour: Of the ancient grains, spelt is the most similar in performance and flavor to modern wheat. It is also the easiest ancient grain to work with. Spelt can be used measure-for-measure with wheat to produce delicious baked goods and breads and is easily purchased in its whole grain form. The Vita Spelt brand offers excellent whole grain spelt flour and white spelt flour. The white spelt is sifted and never bleached.

Rye: With a long historical tradition, rye is especially well-suited to sourdough. Rye makes an incredibly easy and strong sourdough starter. As with the grains discussed above, some people that cannot tolerate modern wheat find that they can eat rye, but it does contain gluten so it's not for those with a wheat allergy or celiac disease. Rye is different from wheat in taste, texture, and performance. Rye can be challenging to work with, but it produces flavorful, nutrient- and mineral-rich breads and baked goods. Rye is very budget-friendly as well. It can be purchased in bulk for nearly half the cost of modern wheat and is about four times cheaper than Khorasan. Rye is the most economical of all the grains covered in this section.

For techniques and recipes using these ancient grains refer to the Ancient Grains section in Homesteading Family's *The Art of Homemade Bread Masterclass.*

Go to **www.homesteadingfamily.com** for more info.

THE ART OF GLUTEN-FREE HOMEMADE BREAD

4. Gluten-Free Flours and Their Purpose

The first step to baking great gluten free breads and baked goods is truly understanding the flours that you are working with. What does each type of flour contribute to the overall mix? What does it taste like? Where can you get it? Here is a run down of some common and not-so-common flours:

Almond Flour: High in protein and healthy fats, almond flour is a good option for adding more protein to your baked goods. With a slightly sweet and nutty flavor, almond flour can improve the taste of other gluten-free grains or starches that can be rather bland on their own. You can purchase almond flour or make your own by blending blanched almonds in the food processor.

Amaranth Flour: Amaranth is a seed native to the Americas. Like quinoa, it comes in many colors, from creamy white to black. Most amaranth is honey-colored. This grain-like seed is high in protein, fiber, B-vitamins, minerals, calcium, and iron. It is ground to produce a flour that has a mild, almost nutty flavor. The flour produces moist pudding-like baked goods when used alone. Amaranth produces excellent results when used as 25%-50% of the total flour in a baking recipe and works well for breading also. Amaranth is prone to rancidity, so smell and taste your flour before you bake with it. If buying from a local store, ask when it was ground (if they grind on-site) or ask if they know when they received the shipment. Home grinding is not recommended as the seed is so small that it falls through most home grinders. You can grind small amounts in a spice mill, coffee grinder, or VitaMix, or you can search for fresh flour online. Freeze purchased flour in airtight containers. Puffed amaranth is a good option if you don't have any options for sourcing fresh flour as it is less prone to rancidity. Never eat uncooked amaranth. It possesses compounds that inhibit nutrient absorption.

Arrowroot Flour: Arrowroot is a white, silky powder very similar in texture to cornstarch. It offers little nutrition but functions as a lightener for baked goods made with other nutrient-dense flours. It browns well and can be used as a coating or breading. Arrowroot is an excellent thickener and can be used in place of cornstarch. Use it as 25% of the total flour in baking combinations to lighten baked goods. Tapioca starch is a good substitute if arrowroot cannot be found. Store arrowroot flour in airtight containers to prevent moisture absorption.

Black Beans: Use cooked, mashed beans to add fiber, protein, and a fudgy texture to baked goods like cakes and brownies.

Brown Rice Flour: Brown rice flour is a useful mild-tasting flour with a slightly sandy texture. Brown rice flour is best blended with other starch or nut flours and is prone to rancidity. Use no more than 50% brown rice for the total flour in your recipe. White rice flour has a longer shelf life than brown rice but is not as nutrient dense. Brown rice flour has more fiber, fat, and protein than white rice flour. You can easily purchase brown rice flour, but milling your own in a grain mill will ensure that it is very fresh.

Buckwheat Flour: Buckwheat is not a grain, but because of its high percentage of complex carbohydrates, the grain-like seeds are used similarly to cereal grains. Buckwheat is best blended with other flours due to its strong flavor. The flavor of white buckwheat is more mild, and all buckwheat works well as breading. Double-check the ingredients on the package of flour you are considering since some manufacturers blend their buckwheat with wheat. Buckwheat flour is readily available commercially.

Cassava Flour: Produced from a root vegetable, this flour is white in color and possesses a mild nutty flavor. Lighter than all-purpose flour, it is a good option for gluten-free baking, but adjustments must be made to the recipe. Due to its high starch content, it absorbs more liquid than other flours, so either use less flour or more liquid in your recipe. Cassava works very well as a single flour in baked goods like cookies and brownies. For cakes or other things that need height and a lighter texture, it is best used blended with other gluten-free flours.

Cashew Flour: see Nut Flours below.

Chickpea Flour: With a mild flavor and color, chickpea flour blends well with other flours and produces yellow-colored baked goods. Though not the best for breading, it is an excellent thickener and protein source when added to baked goods. Use 25% of this flour blended with other flours. Purchase only commercially-ground flour. Dried chickpeas will break the average home grain mill, so do not attempt to grind them yourself. Chickpea flour can often be found in bulk in Indian or Middle Eastern grocery stores. It is often called gram flour. However, be aware that this is not the same as "graham" flour which is wheat-based. If you find legumes hard to digest, start with 1-2 tablespoons of chickpea flour per 1 cup of the flour of your choice and work up from there.

Coconut Flour: This flour has a slightly sweet taste and is high in healthy fats. Made from dried, ground coconut flesh, it contains a high balance of protein, fiber, and carbs. Coconut flour is best used in recipes with eggs and may require extra liquid in some recipes.

Corn Flour: Yellow flour made from dried corn, corn flour is slightly sweet and has a nutty taste that adds depth of texture and flavor.

Corn flour is finer than cornmeal and a different product altogether than masa harina or cornstarch. You can either purchase or mill your own corn flour if you have a mill that can grind flour.

Cornmeal: Similar to corn flour, cornmeal is a coarse flour made from dried corn. However, cornmeal is ground much more coarsely and the finished product is rough and gritty. It is used traditionally in the South in the United States for cornbread. Cornmeal is best used with a blend of other flours rather than alone. It does not possess binding properties so eggs or another binder are needed for successful recipes using this flour.

Cornstarch: Cornstarch is made by refining the starchy endosperm of corn. It has a neutral, bland flavor and is often used to thicken sauces. Cornmeal contains very little nutrition and is nearly all starch. It is best used as a thickener or blended with other flours and used as a breading. While it is easy to purchase, be sure that your cornstarch comes from non-gmo corn.

Fava Flour: This flour is usually made from a blend of garbanzo beans and fava beans. It has a high protein content and a strong "beany" flavor that make it best for use in small quantities. Fava flour is easily purchased.

Lentils and other Legumes: Add Legumes to flour blends in small amounts to increase the protein content. Follow the same graduated flour ratios described for chickpeas when adding to flour blends to avoid the digestibility issues that can come from consuming unsoaked and uncooked legumes.

Masa Harina: This very fine corn flour from corn that has been nixtamalized (or soaked in lime and the hulls removed) is used throughout Middle America. Maseca, which means "dried masa," can be found in the Mexican section of most major supermarkets. If you cannot find it at your regular grocery, check to see if your area has a local Mexican grocery.

Millet: Light ivory in color with a slightly sweet flavor, this tiny seed is low in protein but still quite nutritious. Millet is a good choice in small-to-moderate amounts in quick breads or breads leavened with yeast or sourdough. It is a great grain to buy in bulk and mill at home, as the whole grain is very easily used in other dishes. It can also be purchased as a flour rather easily.

Nut Flours: (other than almond, see almond flour section) Peanuts or cashews can be ground in a blender or a nut or seed mill (not a grain mill!!) in small amounts and then used as 25% of your flour blend. If using nuts with a high oil content, like pecans or walnuts, add a small amount of arrowroot powder or tapioca starch to prevent the ground nuts from clumping. Grind in small amounts and do not store ground nuts as the oils will cause them to go rancid. It is best to err on the side of creating a coarser nut flour since over-processing will cause the nuts to turn into nut butter.

Oat Flour: Oat flour is mild, slightly sweet, and light colored. It has a whole grain flavor and browns well. It can be used in similar proportions as wheat flour. Oats add nice texture to gluten-free breads and baked goods that need more structure. Do not use more than 75% of oat flour or your baked goods will be heavy. Blend rolled oats in a food processor or spice mill to make your own flour. 1 ¼ cups of rolled oats will produce approximately 1 cup of ground flour. Read the labels on oats to ensure that they are produced in a gluten-free facility. Oats are a gluten-free grain but are often processed in facilities that also handle wheat, barley, and rye, so cross-contamination is possible.

Potato Starch and Flour: White, starchy, and flavorless, potato starch and flour brown well and are very similar in texture to cornstarch. Note: Potato flour and potato starch are two different products. Potato starch is made from raw white potatoes. Potato flour is made from cooked potatoes. Both have a high glycemic index. Potato starch is more suitable for most baking as potato flour is heavier and lends a potato flavor to baked goods (which is not always desirable). Potato starch absorbs more moisture and needs a longer rest time to fully absorb all the liquid. It also requires a longer cooking time than some of the other gluten-free starches, so it is best suited for breads or muffins rather than things that bake quickly like cookies.

Quinoa Flour: Quinoa can be white, red, or black, and the white variety is most often made into flour. White quinoa has a nutty flavor and pale color. The seed of this ancient cereal grain produces an excellent quality, nutrient-dense flour when milled at home. Store-bought quinoa flour is expensive and can sometimes have a bitter flavor which is most often the result of the seeds not being properly washed. If you find the flavor of store-bought flour unsatisfactory and you have a grain mill at home, it can be affordable to buy in bulk and grind your own. It is best to use quinoa for no more than 25-30% of your total flour or your baked goods will be heavy and dense. Quinoa makes an excellent and very active sourdough starter, especially in colder temperatures.

Sorghum Flour: Sorghum has a wheat-like taste and a pale brown color. This cereal grain is very nutritious and adds good flavor to otherwise bland gluten-free flour blends. It is readily available commercially.

Soy Flour: Soy can possess a slightly "beany" taste, so it is best used blended in recipes with other strong flavors. Soy adds protein to recipes and works well as a breading when mixed with other starches. Use 2-3 tablespoons of soy flour per 1 cup of flour of your choice. Commercially ground flour that is made from cooked soybeans is preferable because the resulting flour is finer and better tasting than its uncooked counterpart. Soy is also easier to digest if the flour is made from cooked beans. For most people, it is impractical to try and grind this flour at home due to the number of steps (see Chapter 8 for more details on milling this flour at home). Store soy flour in the fridge or freezer to extend its shelf life.

Sweet Rice Flour: This flour is also referred to as glutinous rice flour because of the stickiness of the rice (not because it contains gluten). Sweet rice flour is a starchy grain ground from short grain rice also called "sticky" rice. It has a mild texture and neutral flavor, and it can be used to thicken sauces. Buy this commercially.

Tapioca Flour (aka tapioca starch): With a smooth, silky texture similar to cornstarch, tapioca flour is starch processed from the root of the cassava plant. Tapioca flour differs from cassava flour as tapioca flour is the extracted starch and cassava flour utilizes the entire root. Tapioca flour can be used interchangeably with arrowroot powder. It works well as a breading and thickener. Use it as 25-50% of your total flour to lighten baked goods. Tapioca adds structure, elasticity, and chewiness to baked goods. Sometimes it is also called tapioca starch.

Teff Flour: This flour comes from a very tiny but nutrient-dense ancient grain native to Ethiopia. The grain has a unique flavor and dark brown or ivory color depending on the variety. It is a very dry flour, but ironically it adds moisture to baked goods and lends itself to a tender crumb. Purchase commercially ground flour as the seeds are so small that they will often pass through home flour mills without being ground at all.

Tigernut Flour: Despite its name, tigernut is not a nut. Instead, this flour is made from a root vegetable native to Northern Africa. It has a high nutrient content and possesses a slightly sweet, nutty flavor. Tigernut flour contains natural sugars, so you may want to reduce the amount of sweetener added to your recipe when using it.

White Bean Flour: White beans have a mild flavor and produce a white to ivory flour. This flour is high in protein and helps add structure to breads and baked goods. Because using unsoaked legumes can cause digestive upset in some individuals, use 10% or less of this flour in your total flour content. You will most likely need to mill this flour at home as it can be challenging to find commercially.

White Rice Flour: White in color, white rice flour has a sweet flavor and silky granule-like texture. It is best used as no more than 50% of your flour blend, or the resulting baked goods are likely to be dense and heavy. You can either mill this flour at home or easily purchase the commercially prepared flour.

5. Baking Mixes and Flour Blends

What About Gluten-Free Baking Mixes?

Gluten-free baking mixes can be very convenient. In my experience, mixes which contain gums are not well suited for gluten-free bread, but are wonderful for gluten free baked goods. Typically, they work very well for things like pancakes, cookies, muffins, cakes, and even quick breads, but the gums make non-enriched breads, well, gummy.

Of course, you can make your own mixes. Our recommended mixes for baked goods are in chapter 10 with the Baked Goods Recipes.

So, which commercially available gluten-free mixes are the best? This can largely be a matter of personal preference and taste. Let's review the pros and cons of some of the mainstream brands. (Note: This is not an exhaustive list. As new brands of flours are developed, it's best to use experience as your teacher and give different brands a try to see if you like them. The flour guidelines in this book will help you determine if a mix that you are considering is worth trying.)

Authentic Foods Classical Gluten-Free Blend

Ingredients: Brown Rice Flour, Potato Starch, Tapioca Flour

Simple and sweet on the ingredient list (which is a plus), this flour has the added benefit of being non-GMO. The addition of brown rice flour is beneficial for adding whole-grain nutrition, but the high starch content of the potato starch and tapioca flour is still a consideration when looking for a balanced diet. This blend would result in decent baked goods, but the texture of cookies and muffins might be compromised. Breads might turn out okay if you add psyllium husk and flax meal to improve the texture.

Betty Crocker All-Purpose Gluten-Free Rice Flour Blend

Ingredients: Rice Flour, Potato Starch, Tapioca Starch, Salt, Xanthan Gum

This blend is pretty basic and would lend itself to light baked goods. The flours would likely taste bland on their own and would benefit from the addition of other flavors such as chocolate, fruit, nuts, etc. This blend has a high starch content with no whole grains for added fiber and nutrition. Breads will likely be gummy due to the high percentage of rice flour and the addition of xanthan gum. Notice the added salt which seems unnecessary. Experimentation with reducing the amount of salt used in your recipe would likely be needed if you choose to use this flour blend.

Bob's Red Mill Gluten-Free All-Purpose Flour

Ingredients: Garbanzo Bean Flour, Potato Starch, Tapioca Flour, Sorghum Flour, Fava Bean Flour

The biggest downside to this flour is that baked goods often have an undesirable "beany" taste. It performs well structurally, but cakes and cookies can sometimes be a bit dense.

Bob's Red Mill Gluten Free 1-to-1 Baking Flour

Ingredients: Sweet Rice Flour, Whole Grain Brown Rice Flour,

Potato Starch, Whole Grain Sorghum Flour, Tapioca Flour, Xanthan Gum

This blend is an excellent substitute for wheat all-purpose flour. It has a pleasant taste that mimics (or is sometimes better than) wheat in baked goods. It provides a good structure that is not too dense. Unfortunately, it performs poorly in breads due to the addition of xanthan gum.

Cup4Cup Gluten-Free Flour

Ingredients: Cornstarch, White Rice Flour, Brown Rice Flour, Nonfat Milk Powder, Tapioca Flour, Potato Starch, Xanthan Gum

The high amount of cornstarch in this blend can give baked goods a starchy mouthfeel and result in a compact rather than airy texture.

Cup4Cup Wholesome Flour Blend

Ingredients: Brown Rice Flour, White Rice Flour, Ground Golden Flaxseed, Rice Bran, Xanthan Gum

This flour has a good, nutty flavor but lends itself to heavier baked goods. This is likely due to the added flaxseed which is good for added nutrition but not the best for the texture of things like cookies and muffins. This blend is not recommended for breads due to the addition of xanthan gum.

Gluten-Free Prairie All-Purpose Baking Mix

Ingredients: Oat Flour (partially debranned), Potato Starch, Tapioca Starch, Dried Cow's Milk, Whole Psyllium Husk

This blend would likely make decent baked goods if you can tolerate the oat flour. Debranning the oat improves the texture which would likely be heavy otherwise, but some of the nutrition is removed with the bran.

Glutino Gluten-Free Pantry All-Purpose Flour

Ingredients: White Rice Flour, Potato Starch, Tapioca Starch, Pea Hull Fiber, Acacia Gum, Rice Protein.

This flour wins the prize for the most interesting ingredients – pea hull fiber, acacia gum, and rice protein. This flour has a high starch content, and the added ingredients sometimes contribute "off" flavors to baked goods.

Hodgson Mills Multi-Purpose Baking Mix

Ingredients: Whole Grain Millet Flour, Whole Grain Sorghum Flour, Whole Grain Brown Rice Flour, Xanthan Gum

This blend possesses a whole grain flavor, but the high percentage of millet can result in a slight bitter flavor and dry baked goods. This blend is not recommended for bread due to the addition of xanthan gum.

King Arthur Gluten-Free Measure for Measure Flour

Ingredients: Rice Flour, Whole Grain Brown Rice Flour, Whole Sorghum Flour, Tapioca Starch, Potato Starch, Cellulose, Xanthan Gum, Vitamin and Mineral Blend [Calcium Carbonate, Niacinamide (Vitamin B3), Reduced Iron, Thiamin Hydrochloride (Vitamin B1), Riboflavin (Vitamin B2)]

This flour contains a nice blend of whole grains (brown rice and sorghum). It likely would produce nice baked goods when used for muffins, cookies, or quick breads. However, it may not work well for bread due to the addition of xanthan gum. People who desire no food additives may want to steer away from this blend due to the number of vitamins and minerals added.

King Arthur Gluten-Free Multi-Purpose Flour

Ingredients: White Rice Flour, Tapioca Starch, Potato Starch, Brown Rice Flour, Calcium Carbonate, Niacinamide (B vitamin), Reduced Iron Thiamine Hydrochloride (vitamin B1), Riboflavin (vitamin B2)

This is a good choice for a variety of baking. It provides good structure with no undesirable flavors. The high percentage of rice flour can sometimes lend a slightly grainy texture, but it is not so much as to make it highly objectionable. Due to the sweetness of the rice flours, you may want to slightly reduce the sweeteners if using this blend. People who desire no food additives may want to steer away from this blend due to the number of vitamins added.

NOW Foods Gluten-Free All-Purpose Flour

Ingredients: White Rice Flour, Brown Rice Flour, Tapioca Flour, Potato Starch, Potato Flour, Cellulose

At first glance this looks like it would be a good blend. It contains a whole grain (brown rice flour) and is not purely starch based. However, the addition of potato flour can lend a potato taste to baked goods (unlike potato starch which does not). Also, the addition of cellulose, presumably for added fiber and bulk, may be a negative for some people.

Pamela's Gluten-Free All-Purpose Flour Mix

Ingredients: Brown Rice Flour, Tapioca Starch, White Rice Flour, Potato Starch, Sorghum Flour, Arrowroot Starch, Guar Gum, Sweet Rice Flour, Rice Bran

This blend should work well for most baked goods. The addition of guar gum might create a gummy texture if used for breads. This flour is manufactured in a facility that is certified gluten-free but still processes other allergens, so consult the packaging or online if you have other allergies.

Pillsbury Best Multi-Purpose Gluten-Free Flour Blend

Ingredients: Rice Flour, Potato Starch, Pea Fiber, Tapioca Starch, Xanthan Gum

This flour has a good flavor but poor texture and rise in muffins, cookies, and breads.

Trader Joe's Baker Josef's Gluten-Free All-Purpose Flour

Ingredients: Brown Rice Flour, Potato Starch, White Rice Flour, Tapioca Flour
This flour blend is nice and simple as gluten-free flours go. This is an excellent blend for breads since it does not contain the addition of any gums. This flour does not perform well for other baking like cookies and muffins. However, if xanthan gum were added to muffin and cookie recipes, likely it would be an excellent choice for those as well.

So What's The Bottom Line Best Flour Blend?

For baked goods, our choice is Bob's Red Mill Gluten Free 1-to-1 Baking Flour.

For breads, Trader Joe's Gluten-Free All-Purpose Flour wins. It makes nice breads with the addition of psyllium husk and ground flax meal.

6. Dough Binders and Enhancers

Because gluten-free breads and baked goods lack the structure and stretch that gluten provides, bakers must get creative to replicate that in their products. Below are items that you can add to help your gluten-free flours mimic the structure and texture of wheat-based products.

- **Agar-agar:** This is a vegan product made from seaweed that is used in place of gelatin. It is high in fiber and can add binding properties to gluten-free goods. Too much can make your baked goods overly moist, so add no more than 1 tsp per cup of liquid in your recipe.
- **Carob Bean Gum:** see Locust Bean Gum.
- **Chia Seeds:** These seeds form a gel-like substance when mixed with water. They are a good replacement for gums like xanthan and guar gum. Allow to soak for 10 minutes, but an overnight soak will give you the best results and digestibility.
- **Eggs:** Adding eggs to gluten-free products adds structure and lightness. If you cannot eat eggs, consider adding flaxseeds or chia seeds as an egg substitute.
- **Expandex:** This product is made from tapioca starch and is produced exclusively for the gluten-free market. It mixes with cold water and swells to form a web which mimics the gluten structure in wheat bread. It is flavorless so it will not detract from the flavors of your baked goods, and it has a good mouth-feel which is a plus for the end product. For

baked goods and bread, use ¼ to ¾ cup to replace some of the flour.
- **Flaxseed:** Look for ground or milled flaxseed or flaxseed meal, also called linseed in Europe. It creates a thick, gravy-like liquid when mixed with boiling water. Golden flaxseed is preferred to brown. Brown flaxseeds can contain chlorophyll which is harmless but can add a green tinge to your bread.
- **Gelatin:** This is sourced from animal collagen. It allows liquids to gel which adds stretch to doughs similar to the stretch of gluten. Be sure to look for unflavored varieties if adding this to bread or baked goods.
- **Guar Gum:** Derived from a legume, this gum has great thickening abilities and is very high in fiber. It can add a more starchy feel to baked goods when compared with xanthan gum. It is said that guar gum makes less "gummy" bread than xanthan gum. However, it can cause digestive distress in people with weak or compromised digestive systems if overused.
- **Locust Bean Gum:** This is extracted from the seeds of the carob tree. It is used as a tasteless thickener. This is not the same as carob which is the powdered fruit of the carob tree (not the seed) and tastes similar to chocolate.
- **Non-Fat Milk Powder:** The advantage of adding non-fat milk powder to gluten-free baked goods comes from its function as an emulsifier. It helps the starches to swell and absorb liquid more efficiently. It also helps gluten-free flours mix easier in recipes that have added fat.
- **Pectin:** This is used to thicken jams and jellies. Dried pectin can be added to gluten-free recipes for added structure for things like bread and cakes that need more lift. This product also helps keep baked goods moist.
- **Psyllium Husk Powder:** When psyllium husks are powdered and mixed with liquid, psyllium husk creates a gel-type product that adds lightness and rise. Psyllium is preferred for bread recipes over the addition of gums. The earthy flavor that it imparts is good for products where a whole grain flavor is desired. This is a huge benefit for breads or baked goods

since gluten-free flours can often be bland and tasteless, though the earthy flavor might not be as appreciated in sweets like cookies and muffins.
- **Xanthan Gum:** Made from fermented sugars which are dried and then powdered, xanthan gum increases the viscosity of liquids and makes gluten-free doughs more elastic. Use only a little bit, a teaspoon or less, in most recipes. If too much is used, your product will be slimy or gummy. A package of xanthan gum usually lasts a long time, so it is best stored in the refrigerator. Interestingly, xanthan gum increases the shelf life of foods. It can be sourced from corn sugars, however, so be aware if you have a corn allergy.

THE ART OF GLUTEN-FREE HOMEMADE BREAD

7. Gluten-Free Substitutions

As you know from the previous chapters, additional ingredients are often needed to mimic the gluten in wheat and add lift and stretch to gluten-free baked goods. Eggs, for example, can act as a binder and add lift to gluten-free cakes and muffins. If you cannot use egg, ingredients like psyllium husk, flax meal, or chia seeds can replicate (to some degree) the gluten in wheat or the binding properties of egg. The following ingredient profiles will help teach you when and how to use these ingredients and which ingredients can be substituted for one another.

The recipes in Chapters 10, 11 and 12 are written to be free of as many allergenic foods as possible. Refer to this chapter should you not be able to use one of the ingredients listed in the recipe as written. Granted, every allergy cannot be anticipated, so get your creative juices flowing and experiment on your own if our recommended substitutions do not work for you. Take these recipes and use them as a jumping-off point. Run with them and make them your own. Who knows? You may come up with something better than we did.

Ingredients And Substitutions

All-Purpose Baking Mix

Purpose: Baking mixes like Bob's Red Mill Gluten Free 1-to-1 Baking Flour are used in place of all-purpose wheat flour for baked goods like muffins, cookies, pancakes, and quick breads.

Substitutions: Blends of starch based flours such as potato starch, arrowroot, or tapioca starch and/or light-colored, mild tasting whole grain flours such as sorghum, millet, or oat.

Recipes:
- Pancakes and Waffles
- Muffins
- Quick Breads
- Cookies
- Biscuits and Scones
- Cakes
- Brownies
- Doughnuts and Cinnamon Rolls

Almond Flour

Purpose: Flour with high protein and fat content. Adds nutrition, moist texture, and nutty flavor. Should be used in conjunction with other flours.

Substitutions: Cashew or other nut flours, quinoa flour, white bean flour, or other ground legumes like chickpea.

Amaranth Flour

Purpose: Whole grain flour.

Substitutions: Any whole grain flour such as sorghum, quinoa flour, or millet.

Arrowroot

Purpose: To lighten baked goods.

Substitutions: Tapioca starch.

Recipes:
- Whole Grain Sourdough Loaf
- Whole Grain Sourdough Boule

Baking Powder

Purpose: Leavening agent. Activated by liquid and heat.

Substitutions: Make your own baking powder by mixing 2 tsp of baking soda with 4 tsp of cream of tartar. Otherwise, use another leavening agent like baking soda if your recipe contains an acid. Baking soda requires an acid like vinegar, lemon juice, buttermilk, or sourdough to be activated.

Recipes:
- Muffins
- Quick Breads
- Biscuits and Scones
- Cakes

Baking Soda

Purpose: Leavening agent. Activated by the presence of an acid such as vinegar, lemon juice, buttermilk, , or cocoa powder.

Substitutions: Baking powder, yeast, sourdough. Baking powder is activated by liquid and heat. Yeast is activated when moistened and a caloric sweetener is added and then further activated by the heat when baked. Sourdough is activated when fed flour and water.

Recipes:
- Pancakes and Waffles
- Quick Breads
- Cookies
- Brownies
- Doughnuts and Cinnamon Rolls
- Sourdough Doughnuts

Berries

Purpose: To add flavor, texture, and nutrition.

Substitutions: Berries can generally be used interchangeably. Blueberries, raspberries, strawberries, cranberries, etc. can all be used in baked goods. Cranberries may benefit from being chopped due to their large size and firm texture.

Recipes:
- Muffins
- Quick Breads

Brown Rice Flour

Purpose: Whole grain flour.

Substitutions: Sorghum, millet, oat.

Recipes:
- Basic Whole Grain Loaf
- Buckwheat Boule
- White Sourdough Loaf
- Whole Grain Sourdough Loaf

- Whole Grain Sourdough Boule
- Pizza, Flatbread, Focaccia, Pretzels, Crackers
- Sourdough Muffins

Brown Sugar

Purpose: Sweetener.

Substitutions: White sugar mixed with molasses.

Recipes:
- Cookies

Buckwheat

Purpose: Whole grain flour.

Substitutions: Other whole grain flours such as teff can replace buckwheat as a whole grain flour, but none will mimic the strong, unique flavor of buckwheat (similar to the flavor of rye bread made with caraway seeds).

Recipes:
- Buckwheat Boule
- Pizza, Flatbread, Focaccia, Pretzels, Crackers

Butter

Purpose: Fat. Can add moisture and contribute to a flaky texture in biscuit and scone recipes.

Substitutions: This can depend on the recipe. If the recipe requires a fat that is solid at room temperature so that it can be cut into the dry ingredients (like in biscuits or scones), then you will want to replace butter with another solid fat such as lard, cold coconut oil, or frozen chicken fat. Good quality lard and coconut oil can be used in sweet or savory recipes. Chicken fat should be used in savory recipes.

Recipes:
- Cookies
- Biscuits and Scones
- Doughnuts and Cinnamon Rolls

Buttermilk

Purpose: Liquid. Results in softer baked goods due to added fat content.

Substitutions: Milk soured with vinegar, sour cream, or yogurt.

Recipes:
Pancakes and Waffles
Doughnuts and Cinnamon Rolls

Carob Bean Gum (or Locust Bean Gum)

Purpose: Used as a thickener or binder.

Substitutions: Xanthan gum, guar gum.

Cashew Flour

Purpose: High protein, high fat flour. Nutrient dense. Adds structure and flavor and softens baked goods when used minimally in conjunction with other flours.

Substitutions: Almond flour, other nut flours, quinoa flour, white bean flour, or other ground legumes like chickpeas.

Chia Seeds

Purpose: Binding properties. Can be used as an egg replacement. Substitutions: Egg, psyllium husk, flax meal.

Substitutions: Egg, psyllium husk, flax meal.

Chocolate Chips

Purpose: Flavor.

Substitutions: Carob, white chocolate, peanut butter, cinnamon, butterscotch, or other flavored chips.

Recipes:
- Pumpkin Bread
- Cookies
- Muffins
- Biscuits or Scones
- Brownies

Citrus

Purpose: Citrus like lemon, lime, orange, or grapefruit can add acidity and flavor. Use the juice for recipes that need acidity to activate baking soda or zest to add flavor.

Substitutions: Vinegar.

Recipes:
- Muffins
- Cookies
- Scones

Cocoa Powder

Purpose: To create chocolate flavored baked goods.

Substitutions: Carob powder is similar in flavor.

Recipes:
- Cookies
- Muffins
- Brownies

Coconut Flour

Purpose: Adds mild sweetness and moistness to due the high fat content. The flour should be used in conjunction with other flours to avoid heavy, dense baked goods.

Substitutions: Nut flours.

Cornstarch

Purpose: Lightens and improves browning ability.

Substitutions: Tapioca starch, arrowroot, potato starch.

Eggs

Purpose: Lift and binding properties.

Substitutions: Chia seeds, flax meal, or psyllium husk.

Recipes:
- Pancakes and Waffles
- Muffins
- Quick Breads
- Cookies

- Cakes

Flaxseed Meal

Purpose: Binding properties. Can be used to mimic the structure of gluten in bread.

Substitutions: Egg, chia seeds, or psyllium husk.

Recipes:
- White Sourdough Loaf
- Whole Grain Sourdough Loaf
- Whole Grain Sourdough Boule

Fruit

Purpose: Flavor, texture, added moisture.

Substitutions: Banana, pumpkin, or any other soft puréed fruit can be used to add moisture, bulk, and nutrition to a recipe.

Recipes:
- Muffins
- Cookies
- Biscuits and Scones

Guar Gum

Purpose: Thickener and binder. Best used in quick baked goods. Not ideal for bread. Contained in some baking mixes.

Substitutions: xanthan gum.

Honey

Purpose: Caloric sweetener.

Substitutions: Maple syrup, molasses, agave nectar. Dry sweetener options are sugar, brown sugar, monk fruit (non-caloric), stevia (non-caloric).

Recipes:
- White Sourdough Loaf
- Whole Grain Sourdough Loaf
- Whole Grain Sourdough Boule
- Muffins
- Quick Breads
- Cookies
- Cakes
- Brownies
- Sourdough Doughnuts

Milk

Purpose: Liquid.

Substitutions: Almond, cashew, soy, coconut, oat, hemp milk alternatives. Water, juice, tea, or coffee can be substituted for the liquid called for in a recipe plus 1 Tbsp of fat for each cup of liquid.

Recipes:
- Muffins
- Quick Breads
- Biscuits and Scones
- Cakes
- Brownies
- Doughnuts and Cinnamon Rolls

Milk Powder

Purpose: Adds fat, improves texture and browning.

Substitutions: Use milk powder in place of the liquid called for in a recipe. Add all-purpose flour as an equal substitution for the milk powder called for in a recipe if substituting with liquid milk. For a non-dairy option, add 1 part oil to 2 parts arrowroot powder in place of dried milk powder. For example, if a recipe calls for 3 Tbsp of milk powder, use 2 Tbsp arrowroot and 1 Tbsp oil.

Millet

Purpose: Whole grain flour.

Substitutions: Sorghum, oat, light buckwheat flour.

Recipes:
- Basic Whole Grain Loaf
- Whole Grain Sourdough Loaf
- Whole Grain Sourdough Boule
- Muffins

Molasses

Purpose: Caloric sweetener.

Substitutions: Dark brown sugar + water will mimic the flavor of molasses the best. If using dark brown sugar as a replacement, add ¾ of the amount of molasses called for in the recipe and add 1 tsp of water for every ¼ cup of brown sugar used. Honey, maple syrup, sorghum syrup, or dark Karo syrup can also be used, but the flavor profile will be changed.

Recipes:
- Pumpkin Bread

Monk Fruit

Purpose: Non-caloric sweetener. Cannot be used to activate yeast since it contains no calories.

Substitutions: Stevia or other artificial sweetener.

Nut Butters

Purpose: Adds texture, flavor, fat, and protein.

Substitutions: Peanut, almond, and cashew butters can all be used interchangeably. If you cannot eat nuts, use sunflower butter.

Recipes:
Cookies

Oats

Purpose: Whole grain flour.

Substitutions: Sorghum or other whole grain GF flour.

Recipes:
- Cookies

Oil

Purpose: Fat. Adds moisture or acts as an emulsifier.

Substitutions: For most baking, a flavorless oil like light olive oil, canola, or vegetable oil are acceptable options. Coconut, avocado, nut oils, sunflower, or even extra virgin olive oil can be used as well if the flavor of the oils fits the taste profile of the recipe.

Recipes:
- All bread and baked goods recipes in this book can be baked with any oil of your choice.

Potato Starch

Purpose: Adds structure. Lends itself to a tender crumb. Some mild binding properties.

Substitutions: Cornstarch. Arrowroot or tapioca starch could be used as well, but both are lighter and silkier without the binding properties of potato starch.

Recipes:
- Basic White Loaf
- White Boule
- Whole Grain Loaf
- Baguette/French Bread
- Buckwheat Boule
- White Sourdough Loaf
- Whole Grain Sourdough Loaf
- Whole Grain Sourdough Boule
- Pizza, Flatbread, Focaccia, Pretzels, Crackers
- Sourdough Doughnuts

Psyllium Husk Powder

Purpose: Binder. Adds elasticity & stretch. Ideal for breads.

Substitutions: Flax meal.

Recipes:
- Basic White Loaf
- White Boule
- Whole Grain Loaf
- Baguette/French Bread
- Buckwheat Boule
- White Sourdough Loaf
- Whole Grain Sourdough
- Whole Grain Sourdough Boule

- Pizza, Flatbread, Focaccia, Pretzels, Crackers
- Doughnuts and Cinnamon Rolls

Quinoa Flour

Purpose: Whole grain flour. Heavy. Use in combination with other flours.

Substitutions: Millet, teff, sorghum, oat, brown rice.

Recipes:
- Basic Whole Grain Loaf
- White Sourdough Loaf
- Whole Grain Sourdough Loaf
- Whole Grain Sourdough Boule
- Sourdough Muffins

Salt

Purpose: Adds flavor and tempers yeast activity in breads.

Substitutions: Sea salt is recommended, but a high quality kosher salt will do. And if table salt is what you have, that will work as well.

Recipes:
- All recipes in this book contain salt. Adjust the quantities called for to suit your taste and dietary restrictions. If omitting salt from recipes that contain yeast, reduce the yeast as well.

Sorghum

Purpose: Whole grain flour.

Substitutions: Millet, brown rice, teff, oat, quinoa.

Recipes:
- Basic White Loaf
- White Boule
- Whole Grain Loaf
- Baguette/French Bread
- Buckwheat Boule
- White Sourdough Loaf
- Whole Grain Sourdough Loaf
- Whole Grain Sourdough Boule
- Pizza, Flatbread, Focaccia, Pretzels, Crackers

Sour Cream

Purpose: Adds structure, depth of flavor, moistness to baked goods. Can be used in conjunction with baking soda due to the acid content. Can be used in place of some of the milk called for in a recipe.

Substitutions: Buttermilk, soured milk.

Sourdough

Purpose: Leavening agent.

Substitutions: Yeast with a long fermentation time.

Recipes:
- White Sourdough Loaf
- Whole Grain Sourdough Loaf
- Whole Grain Sourdough Boule
- Buns and Rolls
- Pancakes and Waffles
- Muffins
- Cakes
- Brownies
- Doughnuts

Spices

Purpose: Flavor.

Substitutions: Cinnamon, cloves, nutmeg, garlic, parsley, olives.

Recipes:
- Pumpkin Bread
- Savory Muffins
- Biscuits and Scones
- Doughnuts and Cinnamon Rolls

Stevia

Purpose: Non-caloric sweetener. Cannot be used to activate yeast since it contains no calories.

Substitutions: Monk fruit or other artificial sweetener.

Sugar, Granulated White

Purpose: Sweetener.

Substitutions: Honey, brown sugar, maple syrup. Note that honey burns easier than sugar and does not caramelize in the same way which can cause baked goods to brown faster.

Recipes:
- Nearly every recipe contains some type of sweetener. Use your favorite but pay attention to when a caloric sweetener is needed rather than non-caloric substitutes.

Sweet Rice Flour

Purpose: Mild binding properties. Adds moist texture to baked goods.

Substitutions: White rice flour.

Recipes:
- White Sourdough Loaf

Tapioca Starch or Tapioca Flour

Purpose: Lightens baked goods. Silky, smooth texture. Thickening agent.

Substitutions: Arrowroot powder. Cornstarch can be used, but it lacks the silky quality of tapioca.

Recipes:
- Basic White Loaf
- White Boule
- Whole Grain Loaf
- Baguette/French Bread
- Buckwheat Boule
- White Sourdough Loaf
- Pizza, Flatbread, Focaccia, Pretzels, Crackers
- Sourdough Doughnuts

Teff

Purpose: Whole grain flour.

Substitutions: There is no other GF flour that is quite comparable to teff. Brown rice, sorghum, or oat would probably be the best substitutes, though their textures are all slightly different. Since teff is typically used in small amounts, substituting any other whole grain will usually do.

Recipes:
- Basic Whole Grain Loaf
- Whole Grain Sourdough Loaf

- Whole Grain Sourdough Boule
- Pizza, Flatbread, Focaccia, Pretzels, Crackers

Vanilla Extract

Purpose: Flavoring.

Substitutions: Any other alcohol-based extract will do, based on the flavors you want - almond, hazelnut, etc.

Recipes:
- Pancakes and Waffles
- Muffins
- Quick Breads
- Cookies
- Cakes
- Brownies
- Doughnuts and Cinnamon Rolls

Vegetables, Grated or Pureed

Purpose: Adds flavor, texture, moisture, and nutrition. Also helpful when you have an overabundance of produce.

Substitutions: For grated veggies, use any firm vegetable that is not too high in water content such as carrots or zucchini. Bake and puree very firm produce like pumpkin before using.

Recipes:
- Muffins
- Quick Breads

Water

Purpose: Liquid.

Substitutions: You can typically substitute any other flavored liquid like juice, coffee, etc. measure-for-measure. If adding a liquid that contains fat, like milk or a nut milk, you may want to reduce the amount of fat called for in the recipe.

Recipes:
- In order to accommodate as many food sensitivities as possible, nearly all recipes have been written using water.

White Bean Flour

Purpose: Adds protein and structure.

Substitutions: Another high protein flour like quinoa, almond, or cashew flour.

Recipes:
- Basic White Loaf
- White Boule
- Basic Whole Grain Loaf
- Baguette/French Bread
- White Sourdough Loaf
- White Sourdough Boule

White Rice Flour

Purpose: Adds moist texture to baked goods. Use in blends for all-purpose flour.

Substitutions: Tapioca starch or arrowroot, though these are drier than sweet rice flour.

Recipes:
- Basic White Loaf
- White Boule
- Baguette/French Bread

Xanthan Gum

Purpose: Binder.

Substitutions: Guar gum. Best used in quick breads, muffins, cakes, and cookies. Not ideal for bread.

Yeast

Purpose: Leavening agent.

Substitutions: Sourdough (slower rise time). Can use baking soda or baking powder for quick breads.

Recipes:
- Basic White Loaf
- White Boule
- Whole Grain Loaf
- Baguette/French Bread
- Buckwheat Boule
- Buns and Rolls
- Pizza, Flatbread, Focaccia, Pretzels, Crackers
- Doughnuts and Cinnamon Rolls

Yogurt

Purpose: Adds texture, moisture, and depth of flavor to baked goods. Can be used in place of some of the milk called for in a recipe.

Substitutions: Sour Cream, Buttermilk, Clabber.

Zest from Citrus

Purpose: Flavoring.

THE ART OF GLUTEN-FREE HOMEMADE BREAD

Substitutions: Orange, lemon, lime, or any citrus zest can be used interchangeably based on the flavors desired.

Recipes:
- Muffins
- Cookies
- Quick Breads
- Biscuits and Scones

THE ART OF GLUTEN-FREE HOMEMADE BREAD

8. Gluten-Free Baking Primer

Now that you have a good understanding of the seeds, grains, flours, and binders that are available to you, let's discuss some of the basic baking concepts that you need to master for gluten-free baking and how to get the most nutrition out of your baked goods.

Basic Ingredients

Every recipe, whether gluten-free or gluten-full, contains basic ingredients that are the building blocks to its success. Below are the ingredients that are necessary for successful gluten-free baking.

- **Flour:** Provides structure, substance, and nutrition
- **Sugar:** Sweetens, develops flavors, aids in activating the yeast in breads, and affects browning and caramelization
- **Fat:** Adds moisture and softens texture
- **Eggs:** Works as a binder in gluten-free baking; Adds structure, lift, and improved texture
- **Liquid:** Allows flours to be mixed, blended, and bound together
- **Leavening Agents:** Used to raise baked goods
  - Baking Soda - Reacts with an acid
  - Baking Powder - Reacts with a liquid
  - Yeast - Dormant microbes that activate with a warm liquid

and sweetener
- Sourdough – Mixture of fermented flour and water that raises dough through the metabolic activity of microbes
- **Salt:** Develops flavor and tempers yeast activity

Structure

Each type of baked good has a unique structure that we are trying to achieve. From moist cakes, soft or crispy cookies, and light, airy loaves of bread, the ingredients you use and how you combine them allows you to achieve the structure that you want.

Biscuits

Biscuits are leavened with baking powder to form a light, flaky bread with a soft interior and an exterior that is more crisp. Biscuit dough is formed by cutting small pieces of solid, cold fat into the flour before adding the liquid. When mixing, it is best to work the dough as little as possible. The dough is then folded over itself in layers. This process is called laminating. When baking, the fat melts and the liquid in the fat evaporates in a burst which results in flaky layers in the dough. The colder the dough is kept before baking, the lighter the biscuits will be and the more layers they will have. Biscuits can be pressed out and cut with round cookie or biscuit cutters or even with the mouth of a glass or jar. Alternatively, make drop biscuits by creating a slightly wetter dough and scooping it onto a baking sheet with an ice cream or cookie scoop.

Bread

No gluten-free bread can exactly match the texture and flavor of wheat, but we can come awfully close. You can produce wonderful, delicious, light loaves of bread with just simple ingredients. The breads in this book are all written as lean doughs. This means that the doughs are simple, containing mostly water, flour, and a leavening agent. Enriched doughs often contain milk, eggs, extra fat, and sweetener. The unenriched recipes in this book focus on lean doughs to avoid allergens and to enable most people to eat them. Should you desire, you can always substitute the water called for in the recipe with milk or a milk substitute for a softer bread and added nutrition.

When making gluten-free bread, the mixing order and dough resting are important in achieving the desired results. One of the biggest pitfalls in making gluten-free breads is letting your dough rise too much. Yeast breads are especially prone to this. Room temperature rises should be short since the delicate structure of breads without gluten are not strong enough to hold up to long rise times.

Cakes

Butter, sugar, and eggs typically contribute to the texture of cakes even when wheat flour is used. In gluten-free baking, these ingredients help tremendously in giving the cake lift and creating a soft crumb. If you can't use eggs in your baking, refer to the dough binders and enhancers in Chapter 6. Since these are widely used in gluten-free baking anyway, they are quite helpful when you need to create baked goods without eggs. Also, refer to Chapter 7 where substitutions are discussed.

Cookies

Typically cookies use less liquid and more flour than cakes and the resulting mixture is more firm. Because cookies are baked individually, cookie doughs are generally less complicated and easier to mix than cake batters. In cookie recipes, the butter and sugar are usually combined first, then eggs, liquid next, and finally the dry ingredients such as flour, salt, spices, and leavener. Everything is mixed until just combined. Additions like nuts, coconut, and chocolate chips are added at the end.

Muffins

Muffins are more like mini-cakes in texture. Typically, the wet ingredients are combined, and then dry ingredients are added. Dough should be mixed while very wet and worked minimally for the best texture.

Pie Crusts

Flaky pie crusts are the quintessential achievement of many holiday tables. Pie crusts are made in similar fashion to biscuit dough but with a high percentage of fat and less liquid. The temperature of the fat, water, and dough is crucial to pie crust success: the colder the better. Grated frozen fat (like butter), ice water, and chilling your dough will provide you with the best results. Minimally work the dough and add just as much flour as needed, as too much flour will make for a tough crust. To avoid a soggy crust, brush the crust with an egg wash before baking and pre-bake your crust before adding the filling.

Pizza Dough

Thin crust or deep dish? Everyone has their favorite type of pizza crust. Refer to the base recipe for whole-grain pizza dough in Chapter 11 to start. In gluten-free baking, mixing the dough is easy and thickness is entirely up to your preference.

Quick Breads

When attempting to learn to bake, the easiest beginning bread recipes are quick breads. Quick breads are soft, flavored breads that are typically enriched with eggs, milk, fat, and usually sweetened with sugar (though there are many options for substitutions for these ingredients if needed). To make a quick bread, combine the liquid ingredients and then add the dry ingredients, mixing the dough just until it comes together. Quick breads benefit greatly from additions like mashed fruit (pumpkin or banana for instance) or grated vegetables like carrots or zucchini. These ingredients add flavor, nutrition, and moisture. Typically baked at a slightly higher temperature than cakes, quick breads get their shape from the support of a loaf pan.

Scones

Scones are basically a sweetened, flavored biscuit. They are made using the same technique as biscuits: cutting a solid, cold fat into the flour before adding the liquid. Once mixed, the dough is then laminated (folded into layers) and cut into round, triangular, or square shapes before baking.

Measuring

These recipes were all tested measuring by weight. For the most accurate replication in your own baking, use a kitchen scale. Believe it or not, measuring cups vary in size and measuring 1 cup of flour can vary from baker to baker. If you don't have a kitchen scale, cup and teaspoon measurements are given too. For most recipes, the differences that occur are likely to be minimal, so don't feel compelled to buy a scale if you don't already have one. When measuring with cups or spoons, do not pack or press any of the flour or sugar. All recipes are measured with the measuring cup roughly level.

Whether you are using weight or volume measures, be sure that you achieve the dough or batter texture that is called out in the recipe. This may mean that you add a little more flour or flour mix than is called for until you get the correct texture.

Equipment

Aside from the ease and benefit of a kitchen scale (which is optional), none of these recipes require any special equipment that you aren't likely to have in your kitchen. Bread pans, muffin tins, muffin cup liners, baking sheets, measuring cups and spoons, mixing bowls, a whisk, and a rubber spatula are all that is required to make the majority of these recipes. Some of the more specialized recipes, like the baguettes or French bread, benefit from having special baking pans to achieve the best results, but even then, there are always ways to make do with what you have.

Tips and Tricks Unique to Gluten-Free Baking

- **Kneading** – Not Required!
  In wheat breads, kneading is the process of working the dough to develop the gluten structure. In turn, the gluten structure allows the dough to stretch and lift during baking and helps to give each loaf its shape. It may seem obvious, but because there is no gluten to develop in gluten-free breads, no kneading is required. If you are used to baking with wheat, you may have to retrain your brain in this, but gluten-free loaves just require mixing and shaping. There is no benefit to kneading the dough. Nearly all gluten-free bread recipes create something closer to batters than bread doughs, so you couldn't even knead them if you wanted to.
- **Chill Your Dough**
  Gluten-free doughs and batters benefit from some time in the refrigerator to help the starches gel. If you have trouble getting a recipe to turn out the way you want it to, try chilling your dough to see if that helps.
- **Weigh Don't Measure**
  The most accurate results can be achieved measuring ingredients by weight. If your recipes aren't successful, you might consider investing in a digital kitchen scale so that ingredients can be measured more accurately.
- **Wet Dough**
  Gluten-free baked goods are notorious for being dry and dense. Working with doughs and batters that are more moist can help remedy this. When in doubt, err on the side of wet

dough rather than dry.
- **Rise Times – No Rules Apply Here**
Rise times are all approximate and may vary based on the temperature and humidity of your kitchen, so experience and practice are the best guides here.
  - **Yeast needs one fast rise**
  Watch your yeast breads. They need only one rise and are very easily over-risen. In most kitchens, the bread should rise for no more than one hour. If your bread falls or has a flat top (rather than domed) when it comes out of the oven, it was likely over-risen and needed to be baked sooner.
  - **Sourdough takes longer and you may see very little visible rise**
  Sourdough breads may have very little visible counter rise, but that's okay. Pop them in the oven anyway. They will spring to life once they hit that hot oven.
- **High Altitude Baking:**
Decreased air pressure at high elevations (2000 feet above sea level or above) causes breads to rise more quickly and water to evaporate faster. You may need to make some of the following adjustments to compensate.
  - **Decrease leavening** – Reduce the amount of yeast called for by 25%; reduce baking soda by ⅛ teaspoon for every 3,000 feet of elevation.
  - **Reduce rise times** – Watch your rise times. The lower air pressure will make your dough rise faster than it would at sea level.
  - **Decrease baking times** – Baked goods and breads often bake faster at high altitudes so check your oven 5-7 minutes before the expected end of the baking period.
  - **Increase oven temperature** – If your bread and baked goods fall or are overly moist, experiment with increasing the oven's temperature a bit. This may help set the crumb before the baked goods expand too much so that they can no longer hold their shape.

Digestibility of Gluten-Free Flours

People often choose a gluten-free diet because they are having difficulty digesting wheat. So what should you do if gluten-free flours bother you too? As you can see in Chapter 3, there are a myriad of gluten-free flours to choose from, so it is very likely that you can find a combination of flours that suits your digestive system. However, did you know that there are also ways to make your gluten-free food more digestible?

Let's talk about that for a minute.

Historically, grains, seeds, and nuts were not consumed or baked in their raw forms. Instead, they were soaked, sprouted, or fermented first. So what does that mean for you? It means that you can use these same techniques to help your body digest the foods you eat, elevate the bioavailability of nutrients in your food, and increase the nutrient absorption in your body.

There are three primary ways that you can do this.

Soaking, Sprouting, and Sourdough

Soaking involves submerging your grains or seeds in water and letting them soak overnight (at least 12 hours). After that time, the water is drained, and the item is cooked. Optionally, in the case of breads and baked goods, the flours themselves are allowed to sit for about 12 hours with the liquid added to them. After the soaking time, the remaining ingredients are added and the recipe is completed.

Sprouting starts out with soaking whole grains, nuts or seeds for 12 hours, and then the water is drained and the grains are rinsed. After the water is drained, the grain or seed (which, remember, is a baby plant) is kept moist by frequent rinsing for an additional 12-36 hours until the seeds sprout. The grains or seeds are then dehydrated until completely dry and then milled to make flour.

Sourdough combines ground grain or seeds (aka flours) with water and leaves them to ferment for a period of time to create a "mother" or "starter". This process captures the wild bacteria that naturally occur in the grain, in the air, and in your kitchen environment. These bacteria live and grow in the flour and water mixture. They eat the starches and sugars in the flour, and when they metabolize that food, they give off carbon dioxide, which makes dough rise, and alcohols which give sourdough its tangy, sour taste. The sourdough culture is then added into doughs and batters to introduce the bacteria to a brand new batch of bread or baked goods.

So of the three methods discussed above, which is better?

Well, that depends on what you are making. Honestly, sourdough is the simplest way with the fewest steps and least amount of additional equipment. All the little good bacterias in sourdough not only improve the bioavailability of nutrients and digestibility, but they also often improve the texture of the finished product. Once you have an established sourdough starter that is strong enough to raise bread, you can also add it to any other baked good to increase its digestibility as well.

Soaking is a good option for grains that you intend to cook right away. The challenge with gluten-free baking is that we need to turn all these grains, seeds, and roots into flours. This is where the extra step of sprouting comes in.

Once a grain or legume is soaked, it can be left a little longer to sprout. It is a seed after all. It then needs to be dehydrated and then ground into flour. Two essential pieces of equipment are needed for these additional steps. You need a dehydrator to dry the grains after sprouting and a grain mill to grind them.

Why should you sprout and mill your own grains?

- Increased nutrition and digestibility – Sprouting makes the food easier to digest and activates the germination process, freeing up all the nutrients that would otherwise be saved for the baby plant.
- More cost-effective – If you can buy the grains, legumes, or seeds that you want in bulk, and then soak, sprout, and mill them yourself, you will find that there is a huge cost-savings over buying one little bag of flour at a time. Gluten-free flour isn't cheap. In fact, it's 3 times the cost of buying wheat. But, if you can buy whole grain rice, millet, or buckwheat groats, for example, in bulk and mill them yourself at home, you will see a huge cost-savings.
- More variety of grains – Owning a grain mill will open up a whole new world of variety in grains or seeds. Without a mill, you are entirely dependent on the gluten-free flours that your local health food store or supermarket carries. If you have unusual food sensitivities and cannot use the more commonly available gluten-free flours, milling your own gives you access to a far wider variety of options.

What grains and seeds can I buy in their whole grain form and mill at home?

- Brown rice
- Buckwheat
- Chickpea
- Lentils
- Millet
- Quinoa
- Other beans and legumes
- Oats
- Sorghum
- White bean
- White rice

What grains/seeds canNOT be milled at home?

These grains and seeds cannot be milled at home due to the small size of the grain, the hardness of the grain, or their status as a starch-based root vegetable.

- Amaranth - due to its tiny size
- Teff - due to its tiny size
- Corn - You need a special mill to grind corn due to its extreme hardness. Check the manual of your mill before attempting to grind corn in a home grain mill. Most home mills cannot handle corn and will break if it is attempted.
- Arrowroot - root vegetable
- Tapioca - root vegetable
- Cassava - root vegetable
- Potato - root vegetable
- Soy - Needs to be soaked, cooked, and dried before being milled.
- Coconut - due to high oil content
- Nut flours - due to high oil content
- Tigernut - due to large size and hardness
- Sweet Rice, Sticky, or Glutinous Rice - might gum up your mill due to the texture

What flours can I make at home without a grain mill?

- Almond flour - can be made using a food processor or blender
- Coconut flour - can be made using a high quality blender like a VitaMix
- Soy - can be ground in a high quality blender like a VitaMix after soaking, cooking, roasting until dry, and sifting the flour

How to Soak Grains

Soaking seeds, grains, or legumes neutralizes the phytic acid and other anti-nutrients, unlocking more nutrients for your body. To soak beans, quinoa, millet, or rice, cover the grain, seed, or legume with water and soak overnight. Drain the water and cook the soaked food in a pot of fresh water.

How to Sprout Grains

Follow the steps for soaking as directed above. After soaking overnight, drain the water and cover the bowl with a damp tea towel. Rinse every 12 hours after that or as needed to keep the contents moist until the grain or seeds sprout and tiny tails are visible.

Spread the sprouted grain on dehydrator trays and dry on medium heat until the grain is hard enough that it cannot be dented when pressed on with the edge of your fingernail. Cool the grain completely before transferring to a storage container.

Store your dehydrated grain in airtight containers in a cool place. Grind the grain as needed for your baking purposes. The shelf life of your sprouted grains will be extended if you grind as you need it rather than grinding it all in advance after dehydrating it.

Sourdough is a big topic, so it gets its very own chapter.

9. Gluten-Free Sourdough

How to Make Your Own Sourdough Starter.

Creating a sourdough starter from scratch is a labor of love and requires much patience, but it is also a very simple process that requires only a few minutes of your time each day. While achieving a mature starter may take up to a month, gluten-free starters are often very active and mature much faster than their wheat counterparts. Just follow the process outlined below until your starter passes the "maturity test" that is explained on Day 8. While building a starter from scratch takes more time and work upfront than soaking and/or sprouting, once you have a mature starter to work with, it is the easiest and most flexible method for improving the digestibility and health benefits of your baked goods.

The following instructions for developing a sourdough starter are a modified version of the method taught in the Art of Homemade Bread Masterclass. Because gluten-free flours are more expensive than their counterparts, instructions are given for small feeding amounts. By reducing the upfront cost of the flour investment with smaller feeding portions, this method is designed to make the process of creating a sourdough starter economical and doable for even the busiest households. The overall idea is to feed your starter twice a day for a week. You will choose one day a week as a "Bake Day" where you will bake with a portion of your starter and reserve the remaining starter to continue feeding until it is mature. A mature starter rises or doubles in volume within 3-4 hours. When it shows this level of activity, then you can assume that it is strong enough to raise bread.

Want to see this in action? We cover every step of sourdough starting and baking in video in The Art of Homemade Bread Masterclass. Grab a really special deal on that here:

QR Code

SCAN ME

What flours can I use to make a sourdough starter?

Because making a good loaf of gluten-free bread requires you use multiple flours, it is best to choose 2-3 whole grain flours that you plan to bake with the most often and build your starter with those. While you can certainly make a starter with only one type of gluten-free flour, using multiple flours not only increases the level and diversity of the microbial activity, it gives you the best chance for maximum rise in your gluten-free breads. If you need help deciding which flours to use, please refer to the primer on gluten-free flours in Chapter 3 or scan the flours used in the bread recipes in the Sourdough Bread section of the book for ideas on what flours would work for you. Choose either the flours that you have ready access to or that you know that you feel the best eating. Before choosing, read the list below to learn the few flours that you should avoid when building a sourdough starter. Your starter will respond with the best rise if one-third to one-half of the total amount of flour in your bread recipe is the same as those in your starter. Starters do not like sudden changes in food, so if your starter is made from one set of flours and you use different flours when you mix your bread, your bread's rise may suffer.

Recommended Flours for Building Your Sourdough Starter

Choose 2-3 of the following flours to build your sourdough starter based on your budget and what is easily available for you to purchase.

- **Quinoa flour** is our top recommendation. It has a high level of microbial activity that can even outperform wheat. It is even highly active in cold temperatures which is a huge benefit for the long fermentation times recommended for gluten-free sourdough breads. Quinoa can be expensive and is a heavy flour, so it should be used in minor amounts in your feeding regime. But don't worry, even a small amount will add the beneficial microbes you are aiming for. If you can buy the whole grain and mill your own flour that is preferred to buying the flour already ground.
- **Brown Rice** is an excellent whole grain flour. It is not as heavy as quinoa nor as expensive, and it is a good base flour for many of the following recipes.
- **Sorghum** is another excellent choice. It is light and adds a good taste and texture to baked goods. It is also very active in sourdough.
- **Millet** is a nice whole grain that adds pleasant flavor to many baked goods. It is also relatively inexpensive and easy to find in stores as flour or in whole grain form to mill yourself.

- **Oat** adds a nice texture to baked goods. Just be sure to look for oat flour that is not produced in a facility that also processes wheat products.
- **Buckwheat** is another good whole grain flour. However, it can have a very strong flavor unless you use light buckwheat flour. While some people prefer the strong flavor of buckwheat in bread, it might not be desirable in other baked goods like pancakes and muffins.

Please do NOT use the following flours to feed your starter

- **Nut Flours** - Nuts have a high oil content. This makes them heavy and prone to rancidity. They are not the best choice for building a starter.
- **Legumes** - Legumes can be hard for people with compromised digestive systems to process if they are used in large amounts in gluten-free baking. While beneficial for adding structure and protein to recipes, they should not be used in large amounts. You want to build your starter from flours that will be your base flours in your recipes, and legumes should not be your first choice.
- **Starches** - Gluten-free flours that are primarily starch based such as potato starch, arrowroot, tapioca, and even white rice should not be used to build your starter for the same reason as legumes. While starches are required in gluten-free recipes for lift and texture, they are not high in nutrition and are harder to digest in large amounts. Therefore, choosing a whole grain flour that is nutrient-dense and high in microbial activity is preferred.

Sourdough Starter Supplies

- Quart size jar with plastic lid
- Rubber spatula
- Distilled or purified/filtered water (do not use chlorinated tap water as it can negatively affect the microbial development

of the starter)
- Tablespoon measuring spoon
- 2-3 pounds each of your chosen flours from the list of whole grain flours.

Feeding Instructions

Gather the supplies listed above. Each day you should plan to feed your starter twice. A feeding includes 3 total tablespoons of flour (choosing from the flours listed above) and 2 tablespoons of distilled or purified water, repeated once in the morning and once in the evening.

If you have chosen three different flours, you can feed your starter 1 tablespoon of each flour. If you have chosen to use 2 different flours from the list above, use 1 tablespoon of the more expensive flour and 2 tablespoons of the less costly flour.

Tips for Success:

- If you have other ferments in your kitchen such as kombucha or fermented vegetables, it is best to set your sourdough starter in a location at least 4-6 feet away from those other ferments to avoid cross-contamination of bacteria which can compromise the development of the sourdough microbes.
- If your kitchen is on the cool side, don't worry. Your starter will still develop at any temperature above freezing, it may just take longer. If your kitchen is consistently 65 degrees F (18 degrees C), that's really not a big deal. Just place it in a warm place that is preferably not above 80 degrees F (26 degrees C).
- Avoid direct sunlight. Never place your starter in a sunny window for warmth unless it is in a covered box or container that blocks the sun's rays. Sunlight will deactivate some of the microbes in the starter and it will not fully mature.

Let's get started!

Week 1

Day 1 Morning Feeding:

Mix 3 tablespoons of your chosen flours and 2 tablespoons of water in your quart (liter) sized jar. Stir well with your rubber spatula. Loosely screw on the plastic lid and set the jar in a warm place (70-75° F/21 to 24°C is ideal).

Day 1 Evening Feeding:

Add another 3 tablespoons of your chosen flours and 2 tablespoons of water to your jar, stir well, replace the lid, and return it to its warm spot.

Day 2-7 Morning and Evening Feedings:

Feed 3 tablespoons of flour and 2 tablespoons of water. Stir. Replace lid and set in a warm spot.

Grab your printable sourdough starting cheat sheet here:

SCAN ME

BAKE DAY

Day 8 Morning Feeding:

Remove ½ cup of your starter from the jar that you have been feeding and place in a clean quart sized jar. Feed this ½ cup normally (3 tablespoons of flour, 2 tablespoons of water). Set the new jar in a warm place.

Maturity Test:

If you want to begin testing for maturity, place a rubber band around the girth of the jar with the freshly fed ½ cup of starter and position the rubber band at the level of the starter. Watch your starter over the next few hours. You may notice a little rise above the level of the rubber band. This is how you test for maturity. Once the starter doubles in rise above the level of the rubber band, it is strong enough to make bread. It would be unusual for the starter to be mature after only a week of feedings, but you should be encouraged by any rise and bubbles that you see. If you don't see any, don't worry. Just continue to feed for another week and begin to watch for more and more rise as the week goes on.

Day 8 Bake Day:

Take the extra starter that you have accumulated from the previous week's feeding and bake any recipe that does not depend on the starter for the rise. Pancakes, waffles, muffins, doughnuts, or quick breads are all good options (see Chapter 10 for recipes). If you have a craving for something yummy later in the week, feel free to throw in an impromptu bake day mid-week if you are inclined to do so. The more you use your starter, the more active it will become and the more quickly it will mature. Just be sure that if you remove some starter from your jar to bake with, *always leave at least ½ cup of starter in the jar to continue feeding.* **Never use all of your starter in a recipe.** You always want some left to feed and keep your starter going. If you find that you don't use all of your accumulated starter on your first bake day, simply put the lid on the jar that contains your excess and place it in the fridge until you are ready to bake again.

Week 2

Day 8 Evening Feeding:

Add another 3 tablespoons of your chosen flours and 2 tablespoons of water to your jar, stir well, replace the lid, and return to its warm spot.

Day 9-14 Morning and Evening Feedings:

Feed 3 tablespoons of flour and 2 tablespoons of water. Stir. Replace lid and set in a warm spot.

BAKE DAY

Day 15 Morning Feeding:

Just like last week, remove ½ cup of your starter from the jar that you have been feeding and place it in a clean quart-sized jar. Feed normally (3 tablespoons of flour, 2 tablespoons of water).

Maturity Test:

Test for maturity again by placing a rubber band around the girth of the jar with the freshly fed ½ cup of starter, positioning the rubber band at the level of the starter. Watch your starter for rise over the next 3-4 hours. If the starter doubles in rise above the level of the rubber band, it is mature and you are ready to bake a loaf of bread. If your starter does not double above the level of the rubber band, again, don't worry. Continue to feed your starter for as long as needed until it passes the maturity test.

Day 15, Bake Day:

As you did last week, use the starter that remains from the previous week's feedings to bake something yummy.

Week 3

Day 15 Evening Feeding:

Add 3 tablespoons of your chosen flours and 2 tablespoons of water to your jar, stir well, replace the lid, and return the starter to its warm spot.

Morning and Evening Feedings for Days 16-21:

Continue with feedings as normal.

Week 4

If your starter has not yet tested mature, continue with regular feedings twice a day until you see it double in volume within 3-4 hours. Though unusual, it can take up to 5-6 weeks to achieve a mature starter. This depends on the environmental and microbial conditions in your home. If your starter is not mature yet, just keep going. It will get there.

I have a mature starter! Now what?

First of all, congratulations! Well done on creating your own sourdough starter from scratch. You are now ready to make bread. Choose one of the sourdough bread recipes in the Sourdough Bread section of the book and get ready to bake. Pay attention to the amount of starter required for the recipe that you desire to bake. You may need to feed your starter for a few days to accumulate enough starter, or you can always give your starter a double or triple feeding in order to get the amount of starter that you need to bake with and still have some leftover in your jar to keep feeding. Your goal is to mix your bread after feeding your starter when it is at its peak level of activity. So after you have fed your starter, the best time to mix your bread is 3-4 hours after feeding time when your starter is nice and active. All you have to do now is get ready to BAKE!

Sourdough Starter Questions and Troubleshooting:

"I forgot to feed my starter. Is it ruined?"

No. If you miss a feeding, just continue to feed as normal or give it a double feeding at the next feeding time to make up for it.

"What if I can't feed it exactly every 12 hours? Can I feed it early or a little bit late?"

Certainly. Exact timing is not necessary. The goal is to feed the starter twice a day.

"I noticed lots of bubbles the first few days, but later in the week I hardly saw any. Is it not working?"

Never fear. This is normal in the progression of the development of your sourdough starter. Bubbles are always a good sign as they are evidence that the flours are fermenting properly and that the bacteria are coming alive. But, as the starter increases in volume over the course of the week, you may notice the amount of bubbles and activity lessen and slow. Don't worry. You'll see all that pick up again on bake day when you start off with a fresh jar and begin your weekly feedings again.

"My starter smells very unpleasant. Won't it have an unpleasant flavor as well? I'm not sure I'll want to eat anything made with it."

Strong smells are also normal. Sourdough can go through a myriad of smells as it develops. The developing bacteria can give off a number of smells that we might consider unpleasant. Your starter might smell like alcohol, vinegar, acetone, or even possibly vomit. But don't be alarmed. This is part of the development of the bacteria. Just keep feeding the starter and all that will settle down with time. As the starter matures, the strong smells and flavors will mellow so that by the time your starter is mature and you are ready to bake bread, you will have a lovely, active, pleasantly-sour sourdough starter. As long as your starter does not smell putrid or rotten, just keep on going and enjoy watching your starter grow and mature.

"My starter is very dry. What should I do?"

If you find that your starter is extra dry, simply add a little more water at your next feeding. You should keep your starter about the consistency of a thick pancake batter.

"My starter is very thin and watery. Can I add more flour?"

Yes. If you find that your starter is too thin, simply add some extra flour at the next feeding to thicken it up. Aim for the texture of a thick pancake batter.

"I will be away from home unexpectedly for several days. Will my starter survive? Will I have to start over again?"

You will not have to start again. Sourdough starters are quite flexible. Simply give your starter a double feeding, put a lid on it, and pop it in the fridge. It will wait for you until you get home and you can resume feedings as normal and pick up where you left off.

"Once my starter is mature, do I have to keep feeding it every day?"

No. Once your starter is mature, you do not have to feed it twice a day. You now have the option of keeping your jar of starter in the fridge until you need to bake with it. The cold temperatures will retard the level of activity in your starter and it will wait happily for you for several weeks in the fridge if needed (though it is best for maintenance to take it out and bake with it once per week). If you decide to keep your starter in the fridge, take your starter out of the fridge the night before you want to bake with it so that you can feed it and let it warm up to resume its normal level of activity. Whenever your starter is on the counter, you should feed it twice per day. Otherwise keep it in the fridge until you are ready to bake with it again.

"What if my starter still does not pass the maturity test?"

If you have fed your starter consistently and at the end of four weeks it still does not pass the maturity test, don't despair. It will get there. There are a few things you can do to give it a boost and help it mature faster.

- Bake with your starter more often. The more you use your starter the more active it will become. Just remember to leave ½ cup of starter in your jar to continue feeding.
- Give your starter a double feeding and put it in the fridge for 2-3 days. A period of cold can activate a different set of microbes and make the starter stronger and more active. After a few days in the fridge, take it out and resume normal twice-per-day feedings.
- If you've tried the two steps above and your starter still isn't testing mature, try the maturity test again by taking ½ cup of starter and giving it a double feeding (6 tablespoons of flour, 4 tablespoons of water). Place the rubber band at the level of the starter in the jar and watch the rise over the next 3-4 hours.
- If your home is consistently on the cool side, sometimes a little burst of heat during the maturity test is all the starter needs to kick it into gear. Try the maturity test while placing

your starter on top of your refrigerator, near (but not on) the stove while baking, near a radiator or heating vent, etc. Or if your upstairs is 10 degrees warmer than your downstairs, set it on a dresser in an upstairs bedroom. Get creative and find a spot that is warmer (preferably not above 80 degrees F/26 degrees C) than the place you normally keep it and see what happens.

"My starter has been in the fridge for several weeks, and when I took it out of the fridge it has grey or black liquid on top. Is it ruined?"

No. This liquid is called hooch. It is a type of alcohol that is produced when your starter is hungry. Simply pour that liquid off, and feed your starter for 2-3 days until it resumes its normal level of activity.

"My starter looks like it has mold growing on the top. Do I have to throw it away and start again?"

No. If it is not black or green, it may be Kahm yeast growing on the top of your starter. Simply scrape off the top portion of the starter that contains the yeast, carefully scoop out some of the uncontaminated starter from the center of the jar, place this in a clean jar, and resume feedings as normal. Your starter should resume its normal activity level and be fine after a few days. Even if you do see mold on the top of your starter, sometimes you can still salvage it using the same method: scrape off the top portion that is contaminated, transfer ½ a cup of clean starter to a clean jar, and resume twice-a-day feedings.

"What if my starter dies or someone cleans out my fridge and throws out my starter?"

This can happen and can be devastating after taking the time and effort to create a starter from scratch. The good news is that you can always make it again. To prevent this problem, you can also dry some of your mature starter and create dried sourdough flakes as an added insurance policy. You can keep these as a backup in the event that something happens to your regular starter. To make sourdough flakes, simply take ½ cup of freshly fed starter, spread it on wax paper on top of a cookie sheet, and leave it in a warm area with good air circulation to air dry. Do not place your starter in a dehydrator. The heat will kill the microbes. It needs to be air dried at room temperature. Let it dry for 3-5 days until it is dried evenly all the way through. It should be completely dry and crumbly with no dark areas of moisture at all since moisture will cause mold to form in storage. Crumble up the dried starter and place it in a clean jar with an airtight lid. Store in a dark, cool place. If you ever need it, you can simply reconstitute 2 tablespoons of the dried flakes with some water, resuming twice-a-day feedings for 5-7 days until your starter is fully active again. The dried starter flakes will keep for up to 10 years if they are kept dry and are not exposed to heat.

THE ART OF GLUTEN-FREE HOMEMADE BREAD

Recipes

All-Purpose Gluten-Free Flour Baking Blend	79
Whole Grain Gluten-Free Baking Blend	80
Pancakes	81
Waffles	81
Sourdough Pancakes	82
Sourdough Waffles	82
Raspberry Lemon Muffins	85
Blueberry Lemon Muffins	85
Carrot Cake Muffins	85
Double Chocolate Chip Muffins	85
Blackberry Lime Muffins	86
Blueberry Lemon Sourdough Muffins	87
Banana Chocolate Chip Sourdough Muffins	88
Carrot Cake Sourdough Muffins	89
Savory Garlic Herb Sourdough Muffins	90
Simple Quick Bread	91
Easy Vanilla Icing	92
Pumpkin Bread	93
Chocolate Chip Cookies	95
Double Chocolate Chip Cookies	95
Lemon Drop Cookies	95
Peanut Butter Oatmeal Cookies	95
Oatmeal Raisin Cookies	95
Biscuits	96
Chocolate Chip Scones	97
Cranberry Orange Scones	97
Lemon Raspberry Scones	97

Cinnamon Apple Scones	97
Banana Chocolate Chip Scones	98
Vanilla Cake	99
Vanilla Buttercream Frosting	99
Whipped Cream Frosting	100
Sourdough Vanilla Cake	101
Cake Brownies	102
Sourdough Brownies	103
Troubleshooting and Tips for Cakes & Brownies	104
Cinnamon Rolls	105
Easy Vanilla Icing	106
Cake Doughnuts	108
Sourdough "Discard" Doughnuts:	110
General Mixing, Baking, and Troubleshooting Tips for Yeast Breads	115
Basic White Loaf Bread	118
White Yeast Boule	121
Troubleshooting Tips for Boules	123
Basic Whole Grain Loaf Bread	124
White Baguette or French Bread	127
Buckwheat Boule	131
Buns and Rolls	134
Pizza Crust	135
Flatbread	137
Herbed Focaccia	138
Troubleshooting Tips for Sourdough Breads	143
Troubleshooting Tips for Sourdough Breads	144
White Sourdough Loaf	145
White Sourdough Boule	147
Troubleshooting Tips for Sourdough Boules	148
Whole Grain Sourdough Loaf	150
Whole Grain Sourdough Boule	153
Troubleshooting Tips for Sourdough Boules	154
Sourdough Buns and Rolls	156

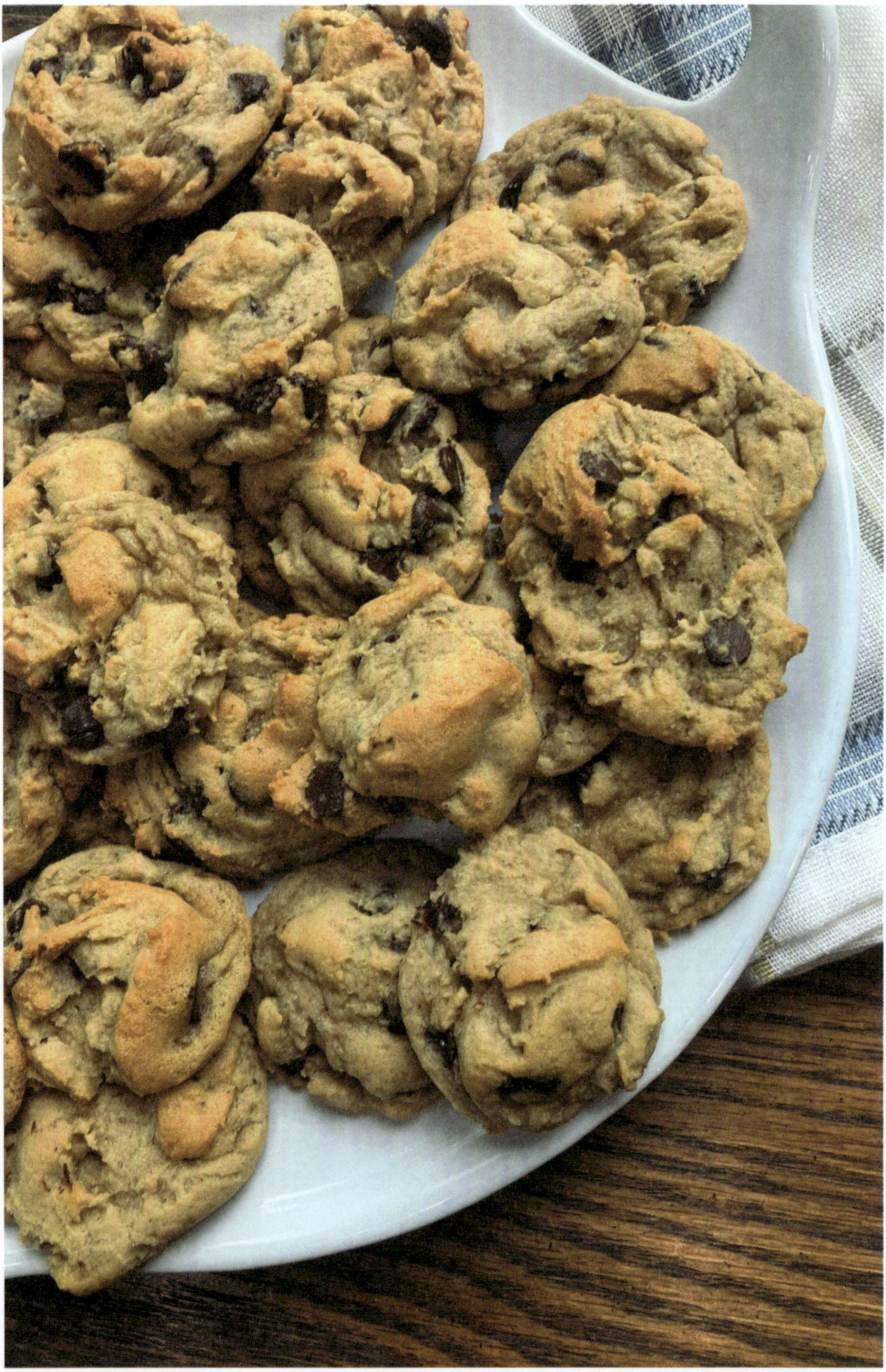

10. Baked Goods Recipes

BAKING BLENDS

The recipes in this section are written to use all-purpose baking mixes like Bob's Red Mill Gluten Free 1-to-1 Baking Flour, or make your own with the following mixes. These mixes can be scaled up or down easily. Consider making a month's worth of a mix and storing it in your pantry until you are ready to use it. Both of these mixes work well for all of the following Baked Goods recipes.

All-Purpose Gluten-Free Flour Baking Blend

Ingredients:
1 part Sweet Rice Flour
1 ½ parts Potato Starch
1 part Sorghum Flour
½ part Tapioca Starch
½ part Millet Flour
½ part Brown Rice Flour
Xanthan Gum (2 tsp for every 5 cups of flour blend)

Directions:
1. Mix all flours and starches together.
2. Add 2 tsp Xanthan Gum for every 5 cups of flour blended.
3. Store in an airtight container in a cool, dark location.

Whole Grain Gluten-Free Baking Blend

Ingredients:
1 part Sorghum Flour
1 ½ parts Potato Starch
1 part Millet Flour
½ part Tapioca Starch
1 part Brown Rice Flour

Directions:
1. Mix all flours and starches together.
2. Add 2 tsp Xanthan Gum for every 5 cups of flour blended.
3. Store in an airtight container in a cool, dark location.

PANCAKES AND WAFFLES

Ingredients:
2 eggs
⅓ cup oil (80ml)
2 ½ cups buttermilk, milk, soured milk, or soured milk alternative (600ml)
½ tsp vanilla extract (2.5ml)
½ tsp salt (3g)
½ tsp baking soda (4g)
2 cups GF Baking Blend (either whole grain or all purpose) or your favorite Gluten Free 1-to-1 Baking Flour blend (390g)

Directions:
1. Whisk together the eggs, oil, milk, vanilla, and salt.
2. Add the flour and baking soda and mix until all the lumps are gone.
3. Lightly grease your preheated skillet or waffle iron.
4. Pour batter into your hot skillet or waffle iron.

Pancakes

Cook until the edges begin to dry and bubbles appear in the center of the pancake.

Waffles

If using a stovetop waffle iron, flip the iron after about 1 minute to cook the other side. If using an electric waffle iron, remove the waffle when the steam lessens. Do not try to open the waffle iron until the full cooking time has elapsed or the waffle will tear and stick.

SOURDOUGH PANCAKES AND WAFFLES

Add ½ cup sourdough starter (125g) to the recipe and use regular milk rather than buttermilk or soured milk.

Ingredients:
2 eggs
⅓ cup oil (80ml)
2 ½ cups milk or milk alternative (600ml)
½ tsp vanilla extract (2.5ml)
½ cup sourdough starter (125g)
½ tsp salt (3g)
½ tsp baking soda (4g)
2 cups GF Baking Blend (either whole grain or all purpose) or your favorite Gluten Free 1-to-1 Baking Flour blend (390g)

Directions:
1. Whisk together the eggs, oil, milk, vanilla, sourdough starter and salt.
2. Add the flour and baking soda and mix until all the lumps are gone.
3. Lightly grease your preheated skillet or waffle iron.
4. Pour batter into your hot skillet or waffle iron.

Sourdough Pancakes

Cook until the edges begin to dry and bubbles appear in the center of the pancake.

Sourdough Waffles

If using a stovetop waffle iron, flip the iron after about 1 minute to cook the other side. If using an electric waffle iron, remove the waffle when the steam lessens. Do not try to open the waffle iron until the full cooking time has elapsed or the waffle will tear and stick.

THE ART OF GLUTEN-FREE HOMEMADE BREAD

Top with your favorite toppings and enjoy!

MUFFINS

Below are recipes for both traditional muffins and sourdough muffins. Take any of the recipes and change the fruits or flavors either to suit your tastes or the ingredients that you have on hand. For example, the Blackberry Lime Muffins below work great as Raspberry Lemon if you happen to have raspberries rather than blackberries on hand. Simply replace the fruit called for and go ahead with the rest of the recipe as written. Play with flavors until you find your favorite combination.

Base Muffin Recipe at a glance:

Yield: 1 dozen muffins.

Ingredients:
¼ cup sugar (50g)
⅓ cup honey (80ml)
2 eggs
6 Tbsp oil (90ml)
¼ cup of water or milk (59ml)
1 tsp vanilla extract (5ml)
½ tsp salt (6g)
1 ¼ cup GF Baking Blend (either whole grain or all purpose)or your favorite Gluten Free 1-to-1 Baking Flour blend (200g)
¼ cup millet flour (30g)
1 Tbsp baking powder (10g)

Directions:
1. Whisk together sugar, honey, eggs, oil, water or milk and vanilla extract.
2. In a separate bowl, whisk together salt, flours and baking powder.
3. Fold the flour mixture into the wet mixture just until combined.
4. Scoop into prepared muffin tins until ⅔ full.
5. Bake at 375°F (190°C) for 20 minutes or until a toothpick inserted in the center comes out clean.

For flavor combinations:
Add extracts with the liquid ingredients.
Add any fruit, chips, or nuts with the dry ingredients.

Muffin Flavor Variations:
Use the following guidelines to adjust the base recipe for the following flavor variations.

Raspberry Lemon Muffins

Add juice of 2 lemons (50g), omit the ¼ cup of water (50g), increase sugar from ¼ cup (50g) to ½ cup (100g), add 1 cup chopped raspberries (120g).

Blueberry Lemon Muffins

Add juice of 2 lemons (50g), omit the ¼ cup of water (50g), increase sugar from ¼ cup (50g) to ½ cup (100g), add 1 cup blueberries (80g).

Carrot Cake Muffins

Add 1 cup grated carrot (120g), 1 tsp cinnamon (2g), dash of cloves.
Banana Chocolate Chip Muffins
Add 2 mashed ripe bananas, ½ cup mini or regular sized semi-sweet chocolate chips, 2 Tbsp brown rice flour (16g).

Double Chocolate Chip Muffins

Add ¼ cup cocoa powder (25g) and omit millet flour (45g), increase sugar from ¼ cup (50g) to ½ cup (100g), add ½ cup mini or regular sized semi-sweet chocolate chips.

Blackberry Lime Muffins

Yield 1 dozen muffins.

Ingredients:
½ cup sugar (100g)
⅓ cup honey (80ml)
2 eggs
6 Tbsp oil (90ml)
Juice of 2 limes (60ml)
Zest of 2 limes
1 tsp vanilla extract (5ml)
1 cup chopped blackberries (150g)
½ tsp salt (6g)
1 ¼ cup GF Baking Blend (either whole grain or all purpose) or your favorite Gluten Free 1-to-1 Baking Flour blend (200g)
¼ cup millet flour (30g)
1 Tbsp baking powder (10g)
1 tsp baking soda (4g)

Directions:
1. Whisk together the sugar, honey, eggs, oil, lime juice, lime zest, vanilla extract, and salt
2. Add the flours, baking powder, and baking soda and fold together until just combined. Gently stir in the fruit at the end.
3. Bake at 375° F (190° C) for 20 minutes.

Blueberry Lemon Sourdough Muffins

Yield: 1 dozen muffins

Ingredients:
⅔ cup sourdough starter, fed or unfed (200g)
½ cup sugar (100g)
¼ cup honey (60ml)
2 eggs
6 Tbsp oil (90ml)
1 tsp vanilla (5ml)
½ tsp salt (6g)
¾ cup GF Baking Blend (either whole grain or all purpose) or your favorite Gluten Free 1-to-1 Baking Flour blend (120g)
2 Tbsp brown rice flour (16g)
1.5 Tbsp baking powder (20g)
1 cup blueberries (80g)
2 Tbsp lemon zest (10g), about 4 lemons

Directions:
1. Combine sourdough starter, sugar, honey, eggs, oil, vanilla, salt and whisk thoroughly.
2. Add the flour and baking powder and fold them in with a rubber spatula. Gently fold in the blueberries and lemon zest.
3. Bake at 375° F (190° C) for 20 minutes.

Banana Chocolate Chip Sourdough Muffins

Yield: 12-16 muffins

Ingredients:
⅔ cup sourdough starter, fed or unfed (200g)
½ cup sugar (100g)
¼ cup honey (60ml)
2 mashed ripe bananas
2 eggs
6 Tbsp oil (90ml)
1 tsp vanilla (5ml)
½ tsp salt (6g)
¾ cup GF Baking Blend (either whole grain or all purpose) or your favorite Gluten Free 1-to-1 Baking Flour blend (120g)
2 Tbsp brown rice flour (16g)
1.5 Tbsp baking powder (20g)
½ cup mini or regular-sized semi-sweet chocolate chips (80g)

Directions:
4. Combine sourdough starter, sugar, honey, bananas, eggs, oil, vanilla and salt.
5. Add the flour and baking powder and mix.
6. Gently fold in the chocolate chips.
7. Bake at 375° F (190° C) for 20 minutes.

Carrot Cake Sourdough Muffins

Yield: 12–14 muffins

Ingredients:
1 cup sourdough starter (270g)
½ cup sugar (100g)
¼ cup honey (60ml)
2 eggs
6 Tbsp oil (90ml)
1 tsp vanilla extract (5ml)
1 cup grated carrot (120g)
1 tsp cinnamon (2g)
Dash of cloves
½ tsp salt (6g)
¾ cup GF Baking Blend (either whole grain or all purpose) or your favorite Gluten Free 1-to-1 Baking Flour blend (120g)
1 ½ Tbsp baking powder (20g)
¼ cup brown rice flour (32g)
2 Tbsp quinoa flour (14g)

Directions:
1. In a bowl, mix together the sourdough starter, sugar, honey, eggs, oil, vanilla extract, grated carrots, cinnamon, cloves and salt.
2. Add the GF flour blend, baking powder, brown rice flour and quinoa flour.
3. Mix thoroughly.
4. Bake 375° F (190° C) for 20 minutes.

Optional: Top with the glaze from the doughnut recipe.

Savory Garlic Herb Sourdough Muffins

Yield: 12-14 muffins

Ingredients:
2/3 cup sourdough starter (200g)
1 tsp sugar (4g)
6 Tbsp oil (90ml)
2 eggs
½ tsp salt (4g)
1 tsp granulated garlic (4g)
2 tsp dried parsley or Italian seasoning (1g)
½ cup chopped olives (20g)
¾ cup GF Baking Blend (either whole grain or all purpose) or your favorite Gluten Free 1-to-1 Baking Flour blend (120g)
1 ½ Tbsp baking powder (20g)
1 Tbsp teff (10g) or 2 Tbsp brown rice (16g)

Directions:
1. In a bowl, mix together the sourdough starter, sugar, oil, eggs, salt, granulated garlic, dried parsley or Italian seasoning and chopped olives with a wooden spoon or rubber spatula.
2. Add the flour and baking powder and mix until just combined, scraping to the bottom of the bowl.
3. Bake 375° F (190° C) for 20 minutes.

Use this recipe as your base to create your own favorite gluten-free quick bread. Any of the muffin recipes above would also bake well as quick breads.

QUICK BREADS

Simple Quick Bread

Yield: 1 loaf. Recipe can be doubled for 2 loaves.

Ingredients:
⅓ cup oil (80ml)
½ cup sugar (100g)
½ cup honey (120ml)
2 eggs
Approximately 1 cup of mashed fruit or 2 cups of fresh whole or chopped fruit
¼ cup milk (59ml)
½ tsp vanilla extract (2.5ml) (or sub almond extract, hazelnut extract, or another favorite flavor)
¾ tsp salt (5g)
1 ½ cups GF Baking Blend (either whole grain or all purpose) or your favorite Gluten Free 1-to-1 Baking Flour blend (215g)
½ tsp baking powder (2g)
1 tsp baking soda (8g)

Directions:
1. Mix the oil, sugar, honey, eggs, fruit, milk, vanilla extract, and salt.
2. Then, add the flour, baking powder, and baking soda and mix until combined. Spoon into a greased loaf pan.
3. Bake at 350° F (176° C) for 1 hour or until a cake tester comes out clean.
4. Cool pans on a wire rack. Frost or ice, if desired.

Optional flavorings: spices, like 1 tsp of cinnamon or ½ tsp of nutmeg, or 1 cup of chocolate chips or nuts

Easy Vanilla Icing

Ingredients:
1/2 cups (55g) powdered sugar aka confectioner's sugar
1 1/2 tsp (7.5 ml) butter, melted
1/2 tsp (2.5 ml) vanilla
1 Tbsp milk (15 ml), or can substitute with heavy cream or half and half

Directions:
1. Combine powdered sugar, melted butter, vanilla and milk in a large mixing bowl.
2. Mix together until smooth.
3. Make sure loaf is cool loaf before icing.

Pumpkin Bread

Yield: 1 loaf. Recipe can be doubled for 2 loaves.

Ingredients:
⅓ cup oil (80ml)
½ cup sugar (100g)
⅓ cup honey (80ml)
3 Tbsp molasses (45ml)
2 eggs
1 cup or about ½ can of canned pumpkin (225ml)
¼ cup milk (59ml)
½ tsp vanilla extract (2.5ml)
¾ tsp salt (5g)
1 ½ cups GF Baking Blend (either whole grain or all purpose) or your favorite Gluten Free 1-to-1 Baking Flour blend (215g)
½ tsp baking powder (2g)
1 tsp baking soda (8g)
½ tsp nutmeg (1g)
1 cup chocolate chips (160g) (optional)

Directions:
1. Mix the oil, sugar, honey, molasses, eggs, pumpkin, milk, vanilla extract, and salt.
2. Then, add the flour, baking powder, baking soda, nutmeg, and chocolate chips if desired and mix until combined. Spoon into a greased loaf pan.
3. Bake at 350° F (176° C) for 1 hour or until a cake tester comes out clean.
4. Cool pans on a wire rack. Frost or ice, if desired.

GLUTEN-FREE COOKIES

Yield: 12-16 cookies depending on size.

Ingredients:
2 cups GF Baking Blend (either whole grain or all purpose) or your favorite Gluten Free 1-to-1 Baking Flour blend (300g)
1 tsp baking soda (7g)
½ tsp salt (3g)
½ cup softened butter (100g)
½ cup packed brown sugar (100g)
¼ cup white sugar (50g)
½ cup honey (118ml)
1 large or 2 small eggs
1 tsp vanilla (5ml)

Directions:
1. Mix the wet and dry ingredients separately.
2. Combine the flour, baking soda, and salt together in a bowl along with any other dry ingredients like cocoa powder or citrus zest if using.
3. Whisk the oil, sugars, honey, eggs, vanilla, and any other wet ingredients in a separate bowl until creamy.
4. Combine the wet and dry ingredients, folding them together with a rubber spatula.
5. Once the dough is combined, add any solid ingredients like chocolate chips and mix.
6. Cover and rest the dough for 30 minutes.
7. Chill dough in the fridge for 2 hours and up to 2 days.

Baking:
8. Preheat the oven to 350° F (176° C).
9. Spoon the cookie dough onto a baking sheet lined with parchment paper. Bake for 8-10 minutes.
10. Remove the pan from the oven and let the cookies sit on the cookie sheet for 5 minutes to set before moving them to a cooling rack.

Add-in Flavors:

Chocolate Chip Cookies
Add 1 cup chocolate chips (180g).

Double Chocolate Chip Cookies
Add 1 cup chocolate chips (180g), replace ¼ cup (50g) of the flour with ¼ cup of cocoa powder (25g), add ½ cup of sugar (100g).

Lemon Drop Cookies

Add 3 Tbsp lemon zest (6g) and 2 Tbsp sugar (20g), sprinkle with powdered sugar after baking.

Peanut Butter Oatmeal Cookies

Add ½ cup quick cooking oats (50g), reduce flour by ¼ cup (50g), add ½ cup creamy peanut butter (120ml).

Oatmeal Raisin Cookies

Reduce the flour by ¾ cups (125g), add 1 cup 5 minute oats (100g), add ⅛ tsp nutmeg and 1 cup raisins (160g).

BISCUITS & SCONES

Biscuits

Ingredients:
2 cups GF Baking Blend (either whole grain or all purpose) or your favorite Gluten Free 1-to-1 Baking Flour blend (300g)
¾ tsp salt (4g)
¼ cup sugar (60g)
1 Tbsp baking powder (10g)
½ stick frozen butter, grated (50-55g)
1 cup milk or water (236ml)

Biscuits:
Reduce sugar to 2 Tbsp (25g).

Directions:
1. Combine the GF flour blend, salt, sugar and baking powder.
2. Grate the butter and cut it into the flour mixture using a pastry cutter or, better yet, your fingers.
3. Work until the dough is dry and crumbly. Work quickly so that the butter doesn't begin to soften.
4. Add any flavoring options (see below) if desired.
5. Add ¾ cup of the milk or water and stir. Add more milk or water only if the dough is too dry. The dough should clean the bowl and be slightly tacky. It should not be dry and crumbly.

Shaping:
6. Once your dough is mixed, gently shape it into a flat disc about ½" (1.5 cm) thick using your hands or a rubber spatula.
7. Wrap the dough in plastic wrap and chill it in the refrigerator for 1 hour.
8. Preheat the oven to 400° F (204° C).

You have several options when it comes to shaping biscuits or scones.

- **Wedges:** You can cut the disc of dough in half, in half again, and then twice more until you have 8 pieces.
- **Round:** Use a round cookie/biscuit cutter to cut out round biscuits or scones. Don't have a cookie/biscuit cutter? Use the mouth of a glass or a jar.
- **Square:** Use a knife or pizza cutter to slice your dough into rows and then into squares.
- **Drop:** Refrigerate your dough immediately after mixing in the bowl without forming a disc shape. At baking time, scoop out your scones with a large cookie scoop or measuring cup to make more free-form rounded biscuits or scones.

9. Place your cut biscuits/scones on a baking sheet lined with parchment paper.

Baking:
10. Bake at 400° F (204° C) for approximately 20 minutes, until the scones or biscuits begin to turn golden brown.

ADD-IN FLAVORS FOR SCONES:

Chocolate Chip Scones
Add 1 cup chocolate chips (100g).

Cranberry Orange Scones
Add 3 Tbsp orange zest (6g), 1 cup dried cranberries (60g), and 2 Tbsp sugar (20g).

Lemon Raspberry Scones
Add 3 Tbsp lemon zest (6g), 1 cup fresh raspberries (120g), and 2 Tbsp sugar (20g).

Cinnamon Apple Scones
Add 1-1.5 cups of finely chopped apples (120g) and 1 tsp cinnamon (2g).

THE ART OF GLUTEN-FREE HOMEMADE BREAD

Banana Chocolate Chip Scones
Add 1 cup mashed ripe bananas (300g), 1 tsp cinnamon (2g), and 1 cup chocolate chips (100g) and reduce milk by ¼ cup (60g).

CAKES & BROWNIES

Vanilla Cake

Yield: Makes one 9" cake.

Ingredients:
½ cup sugar (100g)
3 Tbsp honey (45ml)
2 eggs
½ cup milk or water (118ml)
3 Tbsp oil (45ml)
1 tsp vanilla (5ml)
½ tsp salt (5g)
1 ¼ cups GF Baking Blend (either whole grain or all purpose) or your favorite Gluten Free 1-to-1 Baking Flour blend (220g)
1 Tbsp baking powder (12g)

Directions:
1. Whisk the sugar, honey, eggs, milk/water, oil, and vanilla until combined and creamy.
2. Add the flour, salt, and baking powder and fold in with a rubber spatula until combined.
3. Grease and flour a 9-inch cake pan.
4. Pour batter into the pan and bake at 350° F (176° C) for 20 minutes.
5. Let the cake cool in the pan for 10 minutes, then turn it out onto a cooling rack.
6. Add icing when completely cool if desired.

Vanilla Buttercream Frosting

Yield: Makes enough for a 2 layer cake, or 12 cupcakes

Ingredients:
1 cup softened unsalted butter (227g) (2 sticks)

4.5 cups powdered sugar (540g)
1 Tbsp pure vanilla extract (15ml)
4-5 Tbsp heavy cream or whole milk (60-75ml)

Directions:
1. Mix the butter with an electric mixer or by hand until soft and creamy.
2. Add the powdered sugar and continue to mix together. If using a mixer, scrape down the sides of the bowl with a spatula as needed.
3. When the butter and sugar are combined, add the vanilla.
4. Add in the heavy cream or milk a Tablespoon at a time until desired consistency is reached.

Whipped Cream Frosting

Ingredients:
2 cups heavy whipping cream (474ml)
1 cup powdered sugar (112g)
1 tsp vanilla extract (5ml)

Directions:
In a large mixing bowl, beat the cream with the whisk attachment of an electric mixer until soft peaks begin to form.
Add the powdered sugar and vanilla. Continue beating until stiff peaks form. Use immediately.

Sourdough Vanilla Cake

Ingredients:
1 cup sourdough starter (250g)
½ cup sugar (100g)
3 Tbsp honey (45ml)
2 eggs
3 Tbsp oil (45ml)
1 tsp vanilla extract (5ml)
⅔ cup + 2 Tbsp GF Baking Blend (either whole grain or all purpose) or your favorite Gluten Free 1-to-1 Baking Flour blend (150g)
1 Tbsp baking powder (12g)
½ tsp salt (5g)

Directions:
1. Combine the sourdough starter, sugar, honey, eggs, oil, and vanilla.
2. Add the flour, salt, and baking powder and mix until no lumps remain. Batter should be thick and silky-smooth like a thick pancake batter.
3. Bake at 375° F (190° C) for 20-25 minutes until a cake tester comes out clean.
4. Remove the cake from the oven and let it cool in the pan for 10 minutes before turning it out onto a cooling rack.
5. Cool completely before icing.

Cake Brownies

Ingredients:
½ cup mild tasting oil (118ml)
⅔ cup sugar (125g)
½ cup honey (118ml)
3 eggs
1 tsp salt (7g)
1 tsp vanilla (5ml)
¼ cup milk or water (59ml)
½ cup cocoa powder (35g)
1 ¼ cup GF Baking Blend (either whole grain or all purpose) or your favorite Gluten Free 1-to-1 Baking Flour blend (220g)
1 tsp baking soda (8g)

Directions:
1. Whisk the oil, sugar, honey, eggs, salt, vanilla, and milk together in a bowl.
2. Add the flour, cocoa powder, and baking soda and stir with a rubber spatula until combined.

Baking:
3. Pour batter into a greased 8x8" baking pan and bake at 350° F (176° C) for 40 minutes until the center is set and a cake tester comes out clean.

Sourdough Brownies

Ingredients:
1 cup sourdough starter (250g)
¾ cup sugar (150g)
½ cup honey (118ml)
1 tsp vanilla (5ml)
3 eggs
⅔ cup oil (157ml)
¾ cup cocoa powder (50g)
¾ cup GF Baking Blend (either whole grain or all purpose) or your favorite Gluten Free 1-to-1 Baking Flour blend (135g)
1 tsp salt (7g)
1 tsp baking soda (7g)
½ cup chocolate chips (60g) (optional)

Directions:
1. Whisk the sourdough starter, sugar, honey, vanilla, eggs, and oil together in a bowl.
2. Add in the flour, cocoa powder, baking soda, and salt and stir with a rubber spatula until combined. Fold in chocolate chips if using.

Baking:
3. Pour into a greased 8x8" baking pan and bake at 350°F (176°C) for 35-40 minutes until the center is set and a cake tester comes out clean.
4. For fudgy brownies, remove from the oven when the center has just a very slight jiggle. For cakey brownies, bake until the center is set.

Troubleshooting and Tips for Cakes & Brownies

If you don't like the texture of the brownies consider trying them with your own blend of flours which do not contain rice flour. Sorghum, millet, potato starch, and tapioca are good options with xanthan gum added. If you need to omit the xanthan gum, use psyllium husk instead.

For moist brownies, add a little more oil and omit one egg. For cakier brownies, add an egg and reduce the oil.

This dough can be chilled overnight and baked the next day if desired.

DOUGHNUTS AND CINNAMON ROLLS

Cinnamon Rolls

Ingredients:
1 tsp yeast (4g)
1 tsp sugar (5g) to proof yeast
1 cup warm water (236ml)
2 tsp mild tasting oil or melted butter (10ml)
½ cup buttermilk, soured milk, or milk alternative (118ml)
½ cup sugar (100g)
1 tsp vanilla (5ml)
3 ¼ - 3 ½ cups GF Baking Blend (either whole grain or all purpose) or your favorite Gluten Free 1-to-1 Baking Flour blend (430g)
1 tsp salt (7g)
½ tsp baking soda (7g)
2 Tbsp Brown Sugar (16g)
1 Tbsp Cinnamon (8g)

Directions:
1. Whisk the yeast, 1 tsp of sugar, and warm water together in a mixing bowl.
2. Let the mixture sit for 10 minutes to proof the yeast.
3. After 10 minutes, the yeast should be foamy and bubbly.
4. Now, whisk in the oil, milk, ½ cup sugar, and vanilla.
5. Add the flour, salt, and baking soda and stir to combine.

Shaping:
6. On a floured surface, pat the dough into a rough rectangle about ½ inch (1.25 cm) thick.
7. Brush it with oil and sprinkle it with brown sugar and cinnamon.
8. Roll up the dough from one end, slice into 1 inch rolls, and place the rolls into a greased baking dish.

Rising and Baking:
9. Rise for 1 hour. Brush the top with oil or butter just before

baking. Bake at 350° F (176° C) for 20 minutes.
10. Remove rolls from the oven and cool completely before icing.

Easy Vanilla Icing

Ingredients:
2 cups powdered sugar (224g) aka confectioner's sugar
2 Tbsp (30ml) butter melted
2 tsp vanilla (10ml)
4 Tbsp milk (60 ml) – can substitute with heavy cream or half and half

Directions:
1. Combine powdered sugar, melted butter, vanilla and milk in a large mixing bowl until smooth.
2. Pour over warm rolls and spread.

THE ART OF GLUTEN-FREE HOMEMADE BREAD

Cake Doughnuts

Ingredients:
1 tsp yeast (4g)
1 tsp sugar (5g) to proof yeast
1 cup warm water (236ml)
2 tsp mild tasting oil or butter (10ml)
½ cup buttermilk, soured milk, or milk alternative (118ml)
½ cup sugar (100g)
1 tsp vanilla (5ml)
3 ¼ - 3 ½ cups GF Baking Blend (either whole grain or all purpose) or your favorite Gluten Free 1-to-1 Baking Flour blend (430g)
1 tsp salt (7g)
½ tsp baking soda (7g)
⅛ tsp nutmeg (3g)

SUGAR COATING
½ cup sugar (100g)
2 tsp pumpkin pie spice or cinnamon (5g)

GLAZE
Mix these together until smooth:

- 1 cup powdered sugar (112g)
- ½ tsp vanilla (2.5ml)
- 2 Tbsp milk (30ml) (can also be water/coconut milk if there is a dairy allergy)

Directions:
1. Whisk the yeast, 1 tsp. sugar, and warm water together in a mixing bowl.
2. Let the mixture sit for 10 minutes to proof the yeast. After 10 minutes the yeast should be foamy and bubbly.
3. Whisk in the oil, milk, ½ cup sugar, and vanilla.
4. Add the flour, salt, baking soda, and nutmeg and stir to combine.

THE ART OF GLUTEN-FREE HOMEMADE BREAD

Shaping:
5. Pat the dough into a rough rectangle about ½ inch (1.25 cm) thick.
6. Using a doughnut cutter, biscuit, or cookie cutter, cut large circles of dough. Do not cut out the doughnut hole yet.
7. Transfer the large circles to a baking sheet lined with parchment paper, and then cut out the center hole of each doughnut.

Rising:
8. Place the doughnut holes on the baking sheet as well. Cover with a damp tea towel and let the doughnuts rise for 1 hour.
9. Gently brush the top with oil and bake at 350° F (176° C) for 20 minutes.

Baking:
10. Remove from the oven and while the doughnuts are still warm, immediately dip them in glaze or coat them in butter or oil and dredge them in cinnamon and white sugar.

Sourdough "Discard" Doughnuts:

Yield: Makes approximately 1 dozen large doughnuts, 2 dozen mini doughnuts, or 50 doughnut holes.

These doughnuts use a large amount of sourdough which makes these a good option if you have a lot of sourdough starter to use up.

Ingredients:
3 cups sourdough starter (810g)
¼ cup oil (59ml)
¾ cup tapioca starch (88g)
½ tsp salt (4g)
½ cup honey (118ml)
½ tsp vanilla extract (2.5ml)
½ Tbsp psyllium husk (5g)
¼ cup potato starch (38g)
½ tsp baking soda (4g)

SUGAR COATING
½ cup sugar (100g)
2 tsp pumpkin pie spice or cinnamon (5g)

GLAZE
- Mix these together until smooth:
- 1 cup powdered sugar (112g)
- ½ tsp vanilla (2.5ml)
- 2 Tbsp milk (30ml) (can also be water/coconut milk if there is a dairy allergy)

Directions:
1. In a bowl, add the sourdough starter, oil and tapioca starch and whisk to combine.
2. Stir in the salt, honey and vanilla extract.
3. Add psyllium husk and let the mixture sit for 5 minutes to

THE ART OF GLUTEN-FREE HOMEMADE BREAD

thicken.
4. Next, add the potato starch and baking soda. Stir to combine. The mixture will begin to bubble and foam as the baking soda reacts with the acid in the sourdough. Don't worry, it will settle down in a few minutes. The mixture should be about the thickness of a cake batter.
5. Use a cookie scoop to scoop the batter into a doughnut hole pan, mini muffin pan, or doughnut form pan. If using a doughnut form pan, fill a quart size bag with the batter and snip 2 cm off the end of one corner. Use this as a piping bag to pipe the batter into the doughnut forms. If you don't have doughnut form pans, you can pipe these into doughnut shapes onto parchment paper on a regular cookie sheet, just know that your doughnuts will be flat on the bottom and will not have the same height as they would if you use the shaped pans.
6. Pipe batter into a doughnut form pan.

Note:
If you don't have a doughnut form pan, you can use a baking sheet lined with parchment paper and pipe the doughnuts directly onto the pan.

Baking:
7. Preheat the oven to 400° F (204° C). If using doughnut form pans, place them on a baking sheet in the center rack of the oven.
8. Bake doughnuts for 20 minutes or until the top is just starting to turn golden brown. The undersides will brown faster than the tops so be sure that you check the underside once the tops begin to turn golden or they may have a nice golden top and a dark brown underside.
9. Remove doughnuts from the oven and immediately dip them in glaze or sugar coatings while they are still hot. These doughnuts are best eaten fresh. The flours congeal and tend to be dense the next day.

THE ART OF GLUTEN-FREE HOMEMADE BREAD

11. Yeast Bread Recipes

GENERAL TIPS FOR MIXING & BAKING GLUTEN-FREE BREAD

- **Mixing Order:** The order in which you add the first five or six ingredients for yeast recipes is the most crucial to your end product. The yeast, sugar (or other caloric sweetener), and warm water should all be added together, whisked, and left to rest for at least 10 minutes to give the yeast a chance to proof (become active). After that, the psyllium husk and/or flax should be added, whisked to dissolve, and again left to rest for at least 5 minutes to thicken. The oil or fat should be whisked in at the last. Now your mixture is ready for the flours and salt.
- **Consistency:** Everyone's kitchen is different. You may be baking in a warm, humid kitchen, or a dry, high elevation kitchen, or a thousand options in between. This means that the consistency of your batter will tend to be different than another person's. It is very important that you adjust the flour amount in your recipe to achieve the desired texture. Most of the below recipes will need to be the consistency of thick oatmeal. If your dough is more like a thin pancake batter, slowly add flour until it looks like thick oatmeal.
- **Hand-Mixing:** The texture of the dough for most of the gluten-free breads in this book is more like a thick batter than a dough, so it is fairly easy to mix by hand using a

rubber spatula. A wire whisk can be useful for adding the first few ingredients when you incorporate the yeast and psyllium husk or flax meal, but after that, once the flours are added, the dough becomes too thick and a rubber spatula is the most useful. You can add all the flours and salt and mix them all together at the same time. Be sure to scrape all the way to the bottom of the bowl several times to get any flour that is hiding down there. Mix through to the middle several times to be sure that there are no clumps of flour hiding. You may have to put in some muscle to mix until the clumps are dissolved. If you have problems with the starches clumping, let the dough rest for 10 minutes to give them a chance to soften and then stir again. You'll find that they will melt and combine quite easily.

- **Using a Mixer:** Start out by using a whisk attachment to incorporate the psyllium husk and flax, and then switch to the paddle when adding the flours. Add the flours one at a time, allowing them to incorporate before adding the next one. Be sure to stop and scrape to the bottom of the bowl several times.
- **No-Knead Method:** Because there is no gluten to develop in gluten-free breads, they are easier to mix than wheat-based breads, and kneading is not necessary. Mixing thoroughly either using your rubber spatula or your mixer is all that is necessary.
- **Shaping:** If you have ever baked wheat bread, you know that shaping the bread, whether yeast or sourdough, is a crucial step to how the bread looks and rises in the end. This skill is also simpler with gluten-free bread. There is no gluten or tension to develop like there is in wheat bread, so most of the shaping is done by your baking vessel, usually either a loaf pan or Dutch oven. There is no need to go through the extra steps to shape the dough. Check the instructions for each loaf for specifics on shaping tips.
- **Dry Dough:** If you are mixing and thinking that your dough is too dry, don't add more water. Keep stirring. It takes gluten-free dough a little longer to fully combine and

absorb all the liquid. Keep stirring or give the dough a rest and then stir again. With the exception of the buckwheat and French bread loaves, all of these doughs are more like a batter than a dough. Because the flour absorbs liquid more slowly, it's easy to think that your dough is going to be too dry and will need more water. Fully mix it and let it rest before adding any more liquid and then add water slowly, 1 Tbsp at a time. See below for instructions on adding more liquid if you live in a dry climate.

- **Dry Climates:** If you live in a desert climate with low humidity, your recipes may need more liquid than what is called for. It doesn't take much to compensate. Start with adjusting the liquid up by 5% (about ⅛ cup (25g) for most yeast loaves).
- **High Altitude:** If you live above 2,000 feet elevation, you may need to do some experimenting and adjust your recipes. This is especially the case with bread. Because of the decreased air pressure at higher elevations, gasses expand more quickly and your bread will rise faster. To compensate for this, use less leavening (yeast or sourdough) and decrease your rise times. High altitude climates can be dry and water also boils more quickly at higher altitudes which causes it to evaporate faster, so you may need to add more liquid than what is called for in the recipe.

General Mixing, Baking, and Troubleshooting Tips for Yeast Breads

- **Types of yeast:** Yeasted breads in this book were all tested using active dry yeast. Instant yeast or rapid dry yeast are also acceptable and have the added advantage of allowing you to skip the proofing step. Fresh yeast (also called wet yeast or cake yeast) is another type of yeast, but it was not tested in the recipes because it is rarely found in stores in the U.S.
- **Adding salt:** Salt can kill yeast if it comes into direct contact.

For this reason, it is best to add salt when you add flours so that the salt doesn't come into direct contact with your yeast mixture. Aside from adding and improving flavors, salt also is needed to temper the yeast activity. Too much yeast can ruin a loaf of gluten-free bread in a hurry since the bonds that lift gluten-free breads are so delicate. If it rises too quickly, gluten-free bread won't be able to hold its shape and will collapse in the oven. The yeast bread recipes in this book are designed to include salt. If you need to reduce the salt in the recipes, you may need to reduce the yeast as well to compensate.

- **Dough that does not rise:** Check the use-by date on your yeast. Yeast does not stay fresh forever. Storage conditions can affect the lifespan of yeast and exposure to heat can reduce its potency. Keep yeast in a cool location if storing at room temperature. If buying yeast in bulk, keep it in an airtight container in the refrigerator or freezer for long-term storage.
- **Dough that rises but then the bread falls in the oven:** This is likely due to your dough being over-risen. This is especially easy to do with gluten-free breads. Rise times can vary depending on the temperature of your kitchen. The warmer your kitchen is (85°+ F/30°+ C) the faster the dough will rise. The cooler your kitchen (<65° F/<18° C) the slower dough may rise. You dough needs to rise anywhere between 30 minutes if your kitchen is warm to 1.5-2 hours if your kitchen is cool. Most dough will rise and be ready to bake within an hour if your kitchen temperature is in the 70-75° F/21-24° C range. If you aren't sure, it is better to err on the side of the dough under-risen rather than over-risen.
- **Dough that is over-risen:** Gluten-free loaves hold their rise delicately because they don't have the stretch and structure of gluten. It is easy to tell if your loaves are over-risen. If you push on the risen dough with your finger and it deflates rather than making a gentle dent in that spot, then that loaf has risen too much. If you bake it, it will likely fall and be a dense loaf. If you forget about your dough and find that it is over-risen,

deflate it, reshape, and place it in your loaf pan or bowl to rise again. It may turn out okay, or it may not. It just depends on if there is enough yeast activity left for it to rise a second time and if the structure of the dough will hold up to two rises or not. Gluten-free doughs benefit from using less yeast than you would typically use with wheat. Most wheat breads use 2 teaspoons of yeast. If the same amount was used for a gluten-free loaf, the dough would rise so fast that it would not be able to hold its shape when baked and it would fall in the oven. Gluten-free breads need a slower and gentler rise. Keep an eye on your bread and don't forget to set a timer.

- **Loaf that cracks and breaks open on top:** Of all the problems to have with bread baking, this is the best one. This is a sign that your dough is under-proofed and as a result, you got a great rise once your dough went into the oven. If you want a nice smooth top with no cracks, try increasing your rise time a little. The best way to gauge the rise with gluten-free breads is experience. Once you have baked a recipe a few times, you'll get a feel for how your dough looks when it is fully risen and ready to go into the oven.
- **Bread that does not crack open in the oven:** The flip-side of the problem discussed above is that some people may want their bread to break open for a rustic look. If you desire this and cannot achieve it, try baking your loaf a little sooner in the rise time. If it is a little under-risen, you may get the desired result.

Basic White Loaf Bread

Serves: This recipe makes one loaf in a standard 9x4" or 9x5" loaf pan. It can easily be doubled for two loaves.

Ingredients:
1.5 tsp yeast (7g)
1 Tbsp sugar (15g)
1 Tbsp psyllium husk powder (5g)
1 Tbsp oil (15 ml)
2 ½ cups warm water (600 ml)
2 tsp salt (12g)
¾ cup tapioca starch (100g)
1 cup potato starch (152g)
½ cup white rice flour (75g)
¾ cup sorghum flour (81g)
½ cup white bean flour (52g)

Note: This loaf is easy to mix by hand, but a mixer can certainly be used as well.

Directions:
1. In a bowl, add yeast, sugar, psyllium husk, oil, and warm water.
2. Whisk until the psyllium husk and yeast have dissolved.
3. Let the mixture sit for 10 minutes to allow the yeast to activate. Once the yeast is foamy and bubbly, proceed.
4. Add the tapioca, potato starch, white rice, sorghum, and white bean flours to the bowl. No sifting is necessary.
5. Sprinkle the salt on top of the flours. Mix in the flours with a rubber spatula (or your mixer) until well combined. The mixture should resemble the texture of thick oatmeal.

Shaping & Rising:
6. Pour the bread batter into a buttered or greased loaf pan. Smooth the top of the loaf with your spatula as you would with a quick bread and push the spatula down along the sides

THE ART OF GLUTEN-FREE HOMEMADE BREAD

of the pan about ½ inch (1.25 cm) to just slightly separate the top of the batter from the sides of the pan.
7. Cover loosely with plastic wrap. Let the loaf rise in a warm place until the dough reaches the top of the pan. This may take as little as 30 minutes or as much as 1.5+ hours depending on the temperature of your kitchen.

Baking:
8. Bake at 400° F (204° C) for 60 minutes or until the internal temperature of the loaf registers 210°F (99° C). You may want to turn the pan a few times to be sure that the loaf bakes evenly.
9. Remove the loaf from the pan immediately and cool on a wire rack for 10-12 hours or overnight before slicing.

THE ART OF GLUTEN-FREE HOMEMADE BREAD

White Yeast Boule

This is the same recipe as the Gluten-Free Basic Bread recipe above but it is baked in a Dutch oven to achieve a round boule or peasant loaf shape.

Ingredients:
- 1.5 tsp yeast (7g)
- 1 Tbsp sugar (15g)
- 1 Tbsp psyllium husk (5g)
- 1 Tbsp oil (15ml)
- 2 ½ cups warm water (600ml)
- 2 tsp salt (12g)
- ¾ cup tapioca starch (100g)
- 1 cup potato starch (152g)
- ½ cup white rice flour (75g)
- ¾ cup sorghum flour (81g)
- ½ cup white bean flour (52g)

Directions:
The instructions for mixing this boule (round loaf) are the same as for the loaf above.
1. In a bowl, add the yeast, sugar, psyllium husk, oil, and warm water.
2. Whisk until the psyllium husk and yeast have dissolved.
3. Let the mixture sit for 10 minutes to allow the yeast to activate. Once the yeast is foamy and bubbly, proceed.
4. Add the tapioca, potato starch, white rice, sorghum, and white bean flours to the bowl. No sifting is necessary.
5. Sprinkle the salt on top of the flours. Mix the flours with a rubber spatula (or your mixer) until well combined. The mixture should resemble the texture of thick oatmeal.

Shaping:
6. Tear off a sheet of parchment paper that is about the same width as your mixing bowl.

7. Lightly flour the parchment paper with brown rice flour (do not use white rice or the bottom of your loaf may have a grainy texture).
8. Scrape the dough out of your bowl onto the floured parchment paper and use your rubber spatula to roughly shape the dough into a round ball, smoothing the top and sides with your rubber spatula. The dough will be very sticky and wet. Do not attempt to flour your dough and shape with your hands. You'll end up with a sticky mess and you may have to add so much flour in the shaping process that your dough will be over-floured and dense.
9. After shaping and smoothing your dough, gently pick up the dough by the edges of the parchment paper and transfer it back to your mixing bowl.
10. Cover with plastic wrap or a damp tea towel and leave to rise for 1 hour.

Baking:

11. Once your dough is set to rise, begin preheating your oven with the Dutch oven inside. Preheat the oven to 400° F (204° C).
12. After the rise time is complete, spritz the inside of the parchment paper a few times with a spray bottle filled with water or sprinkle in a few extra drops with your hand. This step is optional, but adding the water will create extra steam which will help your bread rise more and improve the texture.
13. Remove the hot Dutch oven and gently transfer the bread and parchment paper from the bowl into the Dutch oven by lifting it using the edges of the parchment paper.
14. Bake at 400° F (204° C) covered for 40 minutes and then uncovered for 20 more minutes. The internal temperature of the loaf should register 210°F (99° C) when done.

Cooling:

15. Immediately remove the loaf from the pan and remove the parchment paper. Cool bread on a wire rack for 12 hours or

overnight before slicing.

Troubleshooting Tips for Boules

- **Loaves that are too brown on the bottom:** If you find your loaves are getting too dark on the bottom, you can add a stoneware pizza stone or baking sheet to the rack under the Dutch oven to block the heat for the last 20 minutes of cooking time.
- **Loaves that do not brown enough:** After removing the lid from the Dutch oven, remove the loaf from the Dutch oven by picking up the corners of the parchment paper and set it directly on the oven rack for the last 20 minutes of bake time.
- **Not enough oven spring:** If your loaves do not rise as much as you would like, consider spritzing some water in the bottom of the hot Dutch oven before you put the loaf in to add steam and help the rise as the bread bakes. Alternatively, reduce the rise time and bake a little earlier next time.
- **Scores that close or do not open up:** If you decide to score your bread and your scores close up and don't hold their shape during baking, the exterior of your loaf may be too moist. Add extra brown rice flour to the exterior of the loaf before scoring to keep the outside of the loaf dry open and don't bind back to the rest of the dough.

Basic Whole Grain Loaf Bread

Serves: This recipe makes one loaf in a standard 9x4" or 9x5" loaf pan.

Ingredients:
1.5 tsp active dry yeast (6g)
1 Tbsp sugar (15g)
1 Tbsp psyllium husk (5g)
2 tsp salt (12g)
2.5 cups water (600ml)
1 Tbsp oil (15ml)
½ cup sorghum flour (55g)
½ cup tapioca starch (65g)
⅔ cup potato starch (52g)
⅓ cup millet flour (40g)
½ cup brown rice flour (80g)
⅓ cup white bean flour (35g)
¼ cup quinoa flour (28g)
1 ½ Tbsp teff flour (23g)

Directions:
You can certainly use a mixer for this recipe, but it is easy to mix by hand. Add the following ingredients to a medium-sized mixing bowl.

1. Mix the yeast, sugar, psyllium husk, salt, water and oil. Whisk together until the flax meal and psyllium husk are all dissolved. You will see flecks of the psyllium husk in the mixture. It will not completely disappear like sudar does when dissolved in water. The mixture will resemble a slightly thickened sauce.
2. Add the following flours into the bowl- sorghum flour, tapioca starch, potato starch, millet, brown rice flour, white bean flour, quinoa flour and teff flour. They do not need to be sifted.
3. Mix the flours into the liquid using a rubber spatula (or your mixer) until they are all combined. Be sure to incorporate

any lumps of flour and scrape all the way to the bottom of the bowl to get any dry flour that may be hiding there. The mixture will resemble a soft, slightly-gelatinous blob. It should be moldable and hold together but it will be very moist.

Shaping:
4. No kneading is required for this bread. Scrape dough into a greased loaf pan. Take your rubber spatula and gently push down on the edge of the dough all the way along the sides of the loaf pan as pictured below. This will help create a domed shape as the loaf rises and bakes.

Rising:
5. Cover the loaf pan with a damp tea towel and let it rise until it is about ½" from the top of the pan.

Baking:
6. Bake at 400 degrees (204° C) for 50-60 minutes. If you have a covered loaf pan, bake 40 minutes covered and 20 minutes uncovered. The internal temperature of the final loaf should register 200°F - 210°F (93° C - 99° C).

Cooling:
7. Remove the loaf from the pan immediately and place it on a wire rack to cool for 12 hours or overnight if possible.

THE ART OF GLUTEN-FREE HOMEMADE BREAD

White Baguette or French Bread

Serves: This recipe will make 6 baguettes and 2 standard French Bread loaves.

Ingredients:
1.5 tsp yeast (6g)
3 tsp sugar (20g)
3 cups warm water (700ml)
2 tsp oil (10ml)
3 tsp salt (20g)
2 Tbsp psyllium husk (10g)
1 cup tapioca starch (120g)
1 cup potato starch (152g)
⅔ + ¼ cups sorghum flour (100g)
¾ cup white rice flour (113g)
1 cup white bean flour (103g)

Directions:
Due to the larger dough volume of this recipe, a stand mixer is recommended, though you can certainly mix it by hand as well. Just get your muscles ready.
1. In a bowl, add yeast, sugar, and warm water.
2. Mix together and let sit for 10–15 minutes so that the yeast can proof or activate. When you come back to the bowl, you should see that the yeast looks foamy and bubbly.
3. Whisk in oil, and psyllium husk. The mixture should visibly thicken and become somewhat gelatinous looking.
4. Add each of the following flours one at a time, mixing to combine in-between each addition: tapioca flour, potato starch, sorghum, white rice flour, and white bean flour. Be sure to scrape through the center of the dough to the bottom of the bowl to get any dry bits of flour that are hiding under there.

Shaping:

5. Immediately spoon the mixture onto the parchment paper lining the indentations in your baguette or French bread pans. Use your rubber spatula to smooth the surface of the dough into a loaf shape. Once shaped, gently lift the top ¼" of the sides of the dough away from the edge of the loaf pan.
6. If you don't have French bread or Baguette pans, you can make do by lining a rimmed baking sheet with parchment paper and pulling up and folding the parchment paper in the center to make a divider to separate the two loaves (to mimic the shape of French bread/Baguette pans). Then crumple up aluminum foil and lay along either side of the pans under the parchment paper to provide some stability and create a barrier so that the dough doesn't flatten and spread out too much. Shaping the loaves with this make-do method may be difficult so you may find that you need an extra set of hands to hold the parchment paper in place while you shape.

Rise Time:

7. Cover the dough with a lightly-damp tea towel and allow it to rise for 45 minutes to 1 hour. Dough may not visibly increase much in size.

Scoring:

8. If you choose to score, flour the tops of your loaves with brown rice flour and score using a serrated steak knife or lame in the last 15 minutes of the rise time.

Baking:

9. Preheat the oven to 400° F (204° C). Set the French bread pans or baguette pans on a rimmed baking sheet.
10. Spritz the inside of your foil roasting pan with water a few times. Invert the roasting pan so that it sits inverted on top of your baking sheet and acts as a cover for the French bread or baguettes. Covering the loaves will trap steam and help the dough to rise more effectively.
11. Bake covered for 50 minutes. Remove the aluminum pan and

bake for 20 minutes more. Internal temperature should read 200°–210° F (93°–99° C) when tested with an instant read digital thermometer. The bread should be visibly browned.

Cooling:
12. When the bread is done, turn off the oven, crack the oven door, and let the bread rest in the remaining oven heat for 20-30 minutes, watching to be sure that it doesn't get overly brown. This bread is prone to deflating when removed from the oven and cooled too quickly. This added time in the residual oven heat will help further dry the moisture from the bread and allow the crumb to set a little more.
13. Remove the bread from the oven, set the pans on a cooling rack and allow it to cool for at least 30 minutes before moving the loaves.
14. After 30 minutes of cooling on the counter, gently remove the parchment paper from the bread and return the loaves to the French bread/baguette pans to cool for 12 hours or overnight. Due to the curved shape of these bread pans, the bread may deflate and become misshapen if the loaves are cooled on a flat surface, so it is best to leave them in the pans until they are completely cool.

THE ART OF GLUTEN-FREE HOMEMADE BREAD

Buckwheat Boule

This bread could be made in a regular loaf pan or made as a French Bread loaf as well.

Ingredients:
2 tsp sugar (12g)
1.5 tsp yeast (6g)
2 ½ + ⅛ cups warm water (630ml)
1 Tbsp psyllium husk (5g)
1 Tbsp oil (15ml)
2 tsp salt (12g)
¾ cup tapioca starch (90g)
1 cup potato starch (152g)
¾ cup sorghum flour (81g)
½ cup brown rice flour (80g)
1 cup finely ground light buckwheat flour (120g) (or sifted dark buckwheat flour)
1 Tbsp Caraway Seeds (7g) (optional- If you want the flavor of a typical deli rye bread)

Directions:
This dough is more stiff than some of the others, so you might want to use a stand mixer if you have mobility issues or just aren't up for stirring it all up. However, mixing by hand is very doable.
1. Whisk the sugar, yeast, and warm water in a bowl. Let the yeast proof for 10 minutes until it is frothy and bubbly.
2. Add the psyllium husk and oil. Whisk again. Let the mixture sit for 10 minutes allowing it to absorb the water and thicken.
3. Add the tapioca starch, potato starch, sorghum, brown rice flour and buckwheat flour, and then the salt. It is best practice to sprinkle the salt on top of one of the flours rather than directly into the yeast water mixture as the salt can deactivate some of the yeast.
4. Mix all the ingredients using your rubber spatula. If using a stand mixer, add the flours one at a time using the paddle

attachment. Mix until all lumps are incorporated, being sure to scrape to the bottom of the bowl.

Shaping:
5. Cut a piece of parchment paper large enough to cover the top of your bowl. Lay the parchment paper out on the counter and sprinkle with brown rice (or some other light flour).
6. Scoop your dough onto the parchment paper, roughly forming a round ball of dough with your rubber spatula and smoothing the top of the dough as you go. Lift the dough by the edges of the parchment paper and place it back into your mixing bowl. It doesn't even need to be cleaned, just scraped out well.
7. Cover with a lid or damp tea towel if you don't have a lidded bowl.

Rise Time:
8. Let the dough rise covered with the lid or tea towel for 1 hour. Preheat your oven and Dutch oven to 450° F (230° C) halfway through your rise time.

Baking:
9. At the end of the 1 hour rise time, remove your Dutch oven from the hot oven and remove the lid. Be careful. Remember that it is HOT!
10. Remove the lid from your bowl of dough and spritz the inside of the bowl along the edges of the parchment paper with a spray bottle of water 2-3 times.
11. Gently lift the dough by the edges of the parchment paper and place it in the hot Dutch oven. Be as gentle as possible when moving it as you don't want to deflate the dough. Unlike wheat yeast breads, if this dough deflates it is not as easy to reshape and let it rise again. We only really get one chance here.
12. Once your bread is safely in your hot Dutch oven, replace the lid and place your bread in the oven. Reduce the heat to 400° F (204° C). Bake covered for 50 minutes and uncovered

THE ART OF GLUTEN-FREE HOMEMADE BREAD

for 20 minutes. Internal temperature should measure 200–210 degrees F (93–99 degrees C).

Note: If you find that your bread gets too brown on the bottom, place a cookie sheet on the rack under the Dutch oven to block some of the heat from underneath when you remove the lid from the Dutch oven after the first 50 minutes of baking. This will help prevent the bottom from getting too brown.

Cooling:
13. Remove the bread from the oven. Gently lift the bread from the Dutch oven by the edges of the parchment paper and move it directly to a cooling rack.
14. Remove the parchment paper and let the bread cool for a minimum of 12 hours or overnight.

Buns and Rolls

Need rolls for Thanksgiving dinner? Or hamburger buns for that Memorial Day BBQ? Take your favorite bread recipe from this book and simply shape them as buns. It's really easy.

We like the White Yeast Bread Recipe scooped with a ½ cup measuring cup, but feel free to choose a different recipe or size. Mix the dough, and then scoop it out onto parchment paper. Let the buns rise for 1 hour – 1 hour 15 minutes. Bake in an oven preheated to 450° F (230° C). When you put the buns or rolls in the oven, reduce the heat to 400° F (204° C). Bake for 45–50 minutes, turning once at the 30 minute mark to allow for even browning. Cool for 12 hours on a cooling rack or overnight. A one-loaf batch of dough will make six 4–5 inch buns.

OTHER GLUTEN-FREE BREADS

Pizza Crust

Ingredients:
1 tsp sugar (7g)
1 tsp yeast (4g)
1 tsp psyllium husk (2g)
1 tsp oil (5ml)
1 ¾ cups warm water (414ml)
1 tsp salt (7g)
½ cup tapioca starch (60g)
⅔ cup potato starch (102g)
½ cup sorghum flour (56g)
½ + ⅓ cups brown rice flour (120g)
½ cup teff flour (80g)
½ cup buckwheat flour (60g)

Directions:
1. In a mixing bowl, add the sugar, yeast, and warm water. Whisk ingredients together and let the mixture sit for 10-15 minutes to proof. The yeast should become bubbly and foamy.
2. Next, add the psyllium husk and whisk it into the yeast mixture. Let the mixture sit for 5 minutes to thicken.
3. Now add the oil and whisk once more.
4. Measure and add the flours and salt, then stir to combine. The dough should be thick, firm, and hold its shape. It should be able to be shaped into a ball and clean the sides of the bowl.
5. Gently smooth and press the dough onto greased parchment paper to the desired thickness. Cover with a damp tea towel and let it rest and rise for 30 minutes to 1 hour.
6. Bake at 400° F (204° C) for 20 minutes.
7. Remove from the oven and decorate your pizza with your favorite toppings.
8. Return to the oven and bake at 350° F (176° C) for 12-15

minutes more until the toppings are warm and the cheese has melted.

Flatbread

Ingredients:
1 tsp sugar (7g)
1 tsp yeast (4g)
1 tsp psyllium husk (2g)
1 tsp oil (5ml)
1 ¾ cups warm water (414ml)
1 tsp salt (7g)
½ cup tapioca starch (60g)
⅔ cup potato starch (102g)
½ cup sorghum flour (56g)
½ + ⅓ cups brown rice flour (120g)
½ cup teff flour (80g)
½ cup buckwheat flour (60g)

Directions:
1. In a mixing bowl, add the sugar, yeast, and warm water. Whisk ingredients together and let the mixture sit for 10–15 minutes to proof. The yeast should become bubbly and foamy.
2. Next, add the psyllium husk and whisk it into the yeast mixture. Let the mixture sit for 5 minutes to thicken.
3. Now add the oil and whisk once more.
4. Measure and add the flours and salt, then stir to combine. The dough should be thick, firm, and hold its shape. It should be able to be shaped into a ball and clean the sides of the bowl.
5. Gently smooth and press the dough onto greased parchment paper to the desired thickness. Cover with a damp tea towel and let it rest and rise for 30 minutes to 1 hour.
6. After the rest/rise time, bake at 400° F (204° C) for 30 minutes.

Herbed Focaccia

Ingredients:
1 tsp sugar (7g)
1 tsp yeast (4g)
1 tsp psyllium husk (2g)
1 tsp oil (5ml)
1 ¾ cups warm water (414ml)
1 tsp salt (7g)
½ cup tapioca starch (60g)
⅔ cup potato starch (102g)
½ cup sorghum flour (56g)
½ + ⅓ cups brown rice flour (120g)
½ cup teff flour (80g)
½ cup buckwheat flour (60g)

Directions:
1. In a mixing bowl, add the sugar, yeast, and warm water. Whisk ingredients together and let the mixture sit for 10-15 minutes to proof. The yeast should become bubbly and foamy.
2. Next, add the psyllium husk and whisk it into the yeast mixture. Let the mixture sit for 5 minutes to thicken.
3. Now add the oil and whisk once more.
4. Measure and add the flours and salt, then stir to combine. The dough should be thick, firm, and hold its shape. It should be able to be shaped into a ball and clean the sides of the bowl.
5. Gently smooth and press the dough onto greased parchment paper to the desired thickness. Cover with a damp tea towel and let it rest and rise for 30 minutes to 1 hour.
6. After the rest/rise time, drizzle the dough with olive oil and then gently press on the top of the dough with your fingertips to make small indentations.
7. Sprinkle the dough with salt, garlic, herbs, tomatoes, olives, or other favorite toppings.
8. Bake at 400° F (204° C) for 30 minutes.

Optional:
For a sweet version, drizzle with butter and sprinkle with brown sugar and cinnamon before baking.

Gluten Free Crackers

Ingredients:
1 tsp sugar (7g)
1 tsp yeast (4g)
1 tsp psyllium husk (2g)
1 tsp oil (5ml)
1 ¾ cups warm water (414ml)
1 tsp salt (7g)
½ cup tapioca starch (60g)
⅔ cup potato starch (102g)
½ cup sorghum flour (56g)
½ + ⅓ cups brown rice flour (120g)
½ cup teff flour (80g)
½ cup buckwheat flour (60g)

Directions:
1. In a mixing bowl, add the sugar, yeast, and warm water. Whisk ingredients together and let the mixture sit for 10-15 minutes to proof. The yeast should become bubbly and foamy.
2. Next, add the psyllium husk and whisk it into the yeast mixture. Let the mixture sit for 5 minutes to thicken.
3. Now add the oil and whisk once more.
4. Measure and add the flours and salt, then stir to combine. The dough should be thick, firm, and hold its shape. It should be able to be shaped into a ball and clean the sides of the bowl.
5. Gently pat out dough onto a greased sheet of parchment paper until very thin, about 1-2 mm thick.
6. Cover with a damp tea towel and rest for 30 minutes.
7. Brush with oil and season with salt, garlic salt, bagel seasoning, etc.
8. Using a knife or pizza slicer, cut into strips 1-2 inches (5 cm) thick. Then cut again, perpendicular to the first strips, to create squares.
9. Bake at 400° F (204° C) for 15-20 minutes until browned and crisp.

THE ART OF GLUTEN-FREE HOMEMADE BREAD

THE ART OF GLUTEN-FREE HOMEMADE BREAD

12. Sourdough Breads

GENERAL TIPS FOR GLUTEN-FREE SOURDOUGH BREADS

The key to a good loaf of gluten-free sourdough bread is to have a strong starter that doubles in volume within 2-4 hours. If your starter does not double in that amount of time, you could make bread, but you might not get a great rise until it gets a little stronger.

You'll get the best rise from your bread if your sourdough starter is made from more than one of the whole grain flours that are used in the recipe that you are baking. For a more complete discussion of this and making a sourdough starter from scratch, refer to the discussion of sourdough in Chapter 9. A good rule of thumb is to make sure that approximately ⅓ of the total flour in the recipe that you are baking is made up of the same flour(s) that your starter is made of. If you are using a recipe that does not call for the flour that your sourdough starter is made from, refer to the Substitutions section in Chapter 7 to see what flour(s) you might be able to substitute for each other.

Troubleshooting Tips for Sourdough Breads

- **Gummy Loaves:** Using a flour blend that contains xanthan gum can contribute to gummy loaves. Not cooling overnight can cause this as well. If you are still having trouble with gummy loaves, after baking when the loaf's internal temperature

- **No rise or oven spring:** Be sure that you have an active sourdough starter that doubles within 2-3 hours. You also want to be sure that at least ½ cup of the flour used to mix the bread is the same flour that your starter is made from. If you are still having trouble and not getting rise when the loaf is baked, try reducing the rest time after shaping on the counter from 2 hours to 1 hour. Baking with steam can also improve oven spring.
- **Small Loaves:** This recipe is written for loaf pans with a 4.5 x 8" interior. If your loaf pan is bigger than this, try increasing the recipe by half for a larger loaf.

White Sourdough Loaf

Serves: Recipe makes one loaf in a standard 9x4" or 9x5" loaf pan.

Ingredients:
1 cup activated sourdough starter (270g)
2 cups water (500ml)
2 Tbsp honey (30ml)
2 Tbsp oil (30ml)
2 Tbsp flax meal (13g)
1 Tbsp psyllium husk (5g)
2 tsp salt (10g)
⅓ cup brown rice flour (60g)
¼ cup quinoa flour (28g)
⅓ cup tapioca starch (45g)
⅓ cup potato starch (51g)
⅓ cup sorghum flour (36g)
⅓ cup sweet rice flour (52g)
⅓ cup white bean flour (35g)

Directions:
1. In a bowl, add the sourdough starter, water, honey, oil, flax meal, psyllium husk and salt.
2. Mix in a mixer with the beater attachment or use a mixing bowl and wire whisk. Mix until the sourdough starter, psyllium husk, and flax meal are thoroughly dissolved. The mixture should thicken and have the texture of a gravy or sauce.
3. Add the brown rice flour, quinoa flour, tapioca starch, potato starch, sorghum flour, sweet rice flour, and white bean flour.

Note:
Be sure that your starter is made from at least one of the flours used above. If it is not, then substitute either brown rice or quinoa flour with the flour that your starter is made from.

4. Combine the flours either using a paddle attachment if using

a mixer or a rubber spatula if mixing by hand. Mix until all the flour is incorporated, being sure to scrape to the bottom of the bowl. The texture should be thick and soft.

Fermenting Instructions:
5. Immediately after mixing, cover your bowl with the lid and place in the fridge for 24-36 hours.

Baking Day:
6. Remove your bowl from the fridge. Add the dough to a greased loaf pan. Shape the edges of the loaf by pressing down along the edges to slightly separate the dough from the sides of the loaf pan.
7. Cover with a damp tea towel and let the dough rise at room temperature for 1 hour.
8. Preheat the oven to 450° F (230° C).
9. When the oven is hot, place your loaf in the oven and reduce the heat to 400° F (204° C).
10. Bake covered for 50 minutes and uncovered for 25 minutes. If you don't have a covered loaf pan, bake for 50 minutes and check periodically to be sure that your loaf does not over-brown on top. If it is browning too quickly, make a tent of aluminum foil to cover the top and keep it from getting too dark.
11. Bake until the internal temperature reaches 200° F (90° C). Immediately remove the bread from the loaf pan and cool it overnight on a cooling rack.

White Sourdough Boule

This is the same recipe as the Gluten-Free White Sourdough Loaf above with adapted directions should you desire to make it as a boule rather than a loaf shape.

Ingredients:
1 cup activated sourdough starter (270g)
2 cups water (500ml)
2 Tbsp honey (30ml)
2 Tbsp oil (30ml)
2 Tbsp flax meal (13g)
1 Tbsp psyllium husk (5g)
2 tsp salt (10g)
⅓ cup brown rice flour (60g)
¼ cup quinoa flour (28g)
⅓ cup tapioca starch (40g)
⅓ cup potato starch (51g)
⅓ cup sorghum flour (36g)
⅓ cup sweet rice flour (52g)
⅓ cup white bean flour (35g)

Directions:
1. In a bowl, add the sourdough starter, water, honey, oil, flax meal, psyllium husk, and salt.
2. Mix in a mixer with the beater attachment or use a mixing bowl and wire whisk. Mix until the sourdough starter, psyllium husk, and flax meal are thoroughly dissolved. The mixture should thicken and have the texture of a gravy or sauce.
3. Add the brown rice flour, quinoa flour, tapioca starch, potato starch, sorghum flour, sweet rice flour, and white bean flour.

Note:
Be sure that your starter is made from at least one of the flours used above. If it is not, then substitute either brown rice or quinoa flour with the flour that your starter is made from.

4. Combine the flours either using a paddle attachment if using a mixer or a rubber spatula if mixing by hand. Mix until all the flour is incorporated, being sure to scrape to the bottom of the bowl. The texture should be thick and soft.

Fermenting Instructions:
5. Immediately after mixing, cover your bowl with the lid and place in the fridge for 24-36 hours.

Baking Day:
6. Remove your bowl from the fridge to let it warm for 1 hour. Preheat your oven and Dutch oven to 450° F (230° C) for at least 30 minutes before bake time.
7. At the end of the warming period, remove your Dutch oven from the hot oven and remove the lid. Be careful. Remember that it is HOT!
8. Remove the lid from your bowl of dough and spritz the inside of the bowl along the edges of the parchment paper with a spray bottle of water 2-3 times (this will help add some steam which will help your bread to rise).
9. Gently lift the dough by the edges of the parchment paper and place it in the hot Dutch oven. Replace the lid and place your bread in the oven.
10. Reduce the heat to 400° F (204° C). Bake covered for 50 minutes and uncovered for 30 minutes. Internal temperature should measure 200-210 degrees F (93°-99° degrees C).
11. Immediately remove the loaf from the Dutch oven and cool for 12 hours or overnight on a cooling rack.

Troubleshooting Tips for Sourdough Boules

- **Loaves that are too brown on the bottom:** If you find your loaves are getting too dark on the bottom, you can add a stoneware pizza stone or baking sheet to the rack under the Dutch oven to block the heat for the first 50 minutes of cooking time. When you remove the lid from the Dutch oven

for the last 30 minutes of cooking, remove the baking stone as well to let the heat circulate. If your loaf registers 200°F – 210°F (93° C – 99° C) and is as dark as you want it, you can consider reducing the total baking time.
- **Loaves that do not brown enough:** After removing the lid from the Dutch oven, remove the loaf from the Dutch oven and set it directly on the oven rack for the last 30 minutes of bake time.
- **Not enough oven spring:** If your loaves do not rise as much as you would like, consider spritzing some water in the bottom of the hot Dutch oven before you put the loaf in. Steam helps with oven spring.
- **Scores that close or do not open up:** If your scores close up and don't hold their shape during baking, the exterior of your loaf may be too moist. Add extra brown rice flour to the exterior of the loaf before scoring to keep the outside of the loaf dry so that the scores don't close up.

Whole Grain Sourdough Loaf

Serves: Recipe makes one loaf in a standard 9x4" or 9x5" loaf pan.

Ingredients:
1 cup gluten-free activated sourdough starter (270g)
2 cups water (500ml)
2 Tbsp honey (30ml)
2 Tbsp oil (30ml)
2 Tbsp flax meal (13g)
1.5 Tbsp psyllium husk (7g)
2 tsp salt (10g)
⅓ cup brown rice flour (60g)
¼ cup quinoa flour (28g)
⅓ cup arrowroot powder (43g)
⅓ cup potato starch (51g)
⅓ cup sorghum flour (36g)
¼ cup millet (30g)
½ Tbsp teff flour (8g)

Directions:
Though you can certainly use a mixer for this recipe, it is easy to mix by hand.
1. In a medium-sized mixing bowl, add the sourdough starter, water, honey, oil, flax meal, psyllium husk, and salt.
2. Mix with a whisk until the flax meal and psyllium husk are dissolved. The mixture will resemble a slightly thickened sauce.
3. Add the brown rice flour, quinoa flour, arrowroot powder, potato starch, sorghum flour, millet and teff. No sifting is needed.

Note:
Be sure that your starter is made from at least one of the flours used above. If it is not, then substitute either brown rice or quinoa flour with the flour that your starter is made from.

4. When all the flours have been added to the bowl, stir with a rubber spatula until it is thoroughly mixed, being sure to scrape all the way to the bottom of the bowl. Your mixture should resemble a moist, soft, thick batter.

Fermenting Instructions:
5. Immediately after mixing, cover your bowl with the lid and place in the fridge for 24-36 hours.

Baking Day:
6. Remove your bowl from the fridge. Turn out dough onto a floured work surface (brown rice flour works well for this) and shape into a log shape. No kneading is required for this dough.
7. Place the shaped loaf into a greased loaf pan, cover, and let it sit at room temperature for 2 hours. Your loaf will likely rise a little but it may not be very noticeable.
8. At the 2 hour mark, preheat your oven to 450° F (230° C). When you place your loaf in the oven, reduce the heat to 400° F (204° C).
9. Bake covered for 50 minutes and uncovered for 30 minutes.
10. If possible, bake in a covered loaf pan, or place your loaf pan on a rack inside your Dutch oven to create an enclosed baking environment. Baking in a covered loaf pan or in a loaf pan in your Dutch oven will allow you to take advantage of the steam and likely achieve a better rise.
11. If you do not have a covered loaf pan or if your loaf pan will not fit inside your Dutch oven, then you can add steam to your oven by adding ice or water to a metal, heat-proof baking sheet placed on the rack under your loaf pan. Alternatively, you can bake without steam. If baking without steam, bake the bread for 1 hour, checking your loaf every 10 minutes after the 1 hour mark to be sure that it is not getting overly brown.
12. Your loaf is done when the bottom sounds hollow when thumped or when the internal temperature reads between

200°F - 210°F (93° C - 99° C).
13. Let the loaf sit for 5 minutes after being removed from the oven. Then remove it from the pan and place it on a cooling rack.
14. Let the bread cool for 12 hours or overnight. Do not skimp on the cooling time or your loaves will be gummy and gooey inside.

Whole Grain Sourdough Boule

Ingredients:
1 cup activated sourdough starter (270g)
1 ½ cups water (375ml)
1 ½ Tbsp honey (22ml)
1 Tbsp oil (15ml)
2 Tbsp flax meal (13g)
1 Tbsp psyllium husk (5g)
¼ cup brown rice flour (40g)
2 Tbsp quinoa flour (14g)
2 tsp salt (10g)
⅓ cup arrowroot powder (43g)
⅓ cup potato starch (51g)
⅓ cup + 2 Tbsp sorghum flour (50g)
½ Tbsp teff flour (8g)
2 Tbsp millet flour (15g)

Directions:
Though you can certainly use a mixer for this recipe, it is easy to mix by hand.
1. In a medium sized mixing bowl, add the activated sourdough starter, water, honey, oil, flax meal, and psyllium husk.
2. Mix with a whisk until the flax meal and psyllium husk are dissolved.
3. Add the brown rice flour, quinoa flour, salt, arrowroot powder, potato starch, sorghum flour, teff and millet. No sifting is needed.

Note:
Be sure that your starter is made from at least one of the flours used above. If it is not, then substitute either brown rice or quinoa flour with the flour that your starter is made from.

4. When all the flours have been added to the bowl, stir with a rubber spatula until it is thoroughly mixed, being sure to

scrape all the way to the bottom of the bowl. Your mixture should resemble a moist, soft, thick batter.

Fermenting Instructions:
5. Immediately after mixing, cover your bowl with the lid and place in the fridge for 24-36 hours.

Baking Day:
6. Remove your bowl from the fridge. Turn out onto a floured work surface (brown rice flour works well for this) and shape into a round loaf. Line the same mixing bowl with a clean, dry tea towel and flour heavily. Place the loaf upside down in the towel lined bowl (seam side up). Fold over the towel edges and place the lid back on the bowl or cover with another damp tea towel.
7. Let the dough sit at room temperature for 1 hour.
8. Fifteen minutes before the 1 hour mark, preheat the oven and the Dutch oven that you plan to bake in to 450° F (230° C).
9. When the oven is hot, turn the loaf out onto a clean sheet of parchment paper. Spread brown rice flour over the top of the loaf, adding more if there is not enough remaining from flouring the towel. Score deeply with a sharp serrated knife or lame if desired. When you place your loaf in the oven, reduce the heat to 400° F (204° C).
10. Bake covered for 50 minutes and uncovered for 30 minutes.

Troubleshooting Tips for Sourdough Boules

- **Loaves that are too brown on the bottom:** If you find your loaves are getting too dark on the bottom, you can add a stoneware pizza stone or baking sheet to the rack under the Dutch oven to block the heat for the first 50 minutes of cooking time. When you remove the lid from the Dutch oven for the last 30 minutes of cooking, remove the baking stone as well to let the heat circulate. If your loaf registers 200°F - 210°F (93° C - 99° C) and is as dark as you want it, you can consider reducing the total baking time.

- **Loaves that do not brown enough:** After removing the lid from the Dutch oven, remove the loaf from the Dutch oven and set it directly on the oven rack for the last 30 minutes of bake time.
- **Not enough oven spring:** If your loaves do not rise as much as you would like, consider spritzing some water in the bottom of the hot Dutch oven before you put the loaf in.
- **Scores that close or do not open up:** If your scores close up and don't hold their shape during baking, the exterior of your loaf may be too moist. Add extra brown rice flour to the exterior of the loaf before scoring to keep the outside of the loaf dry so that the scores don't close up.

Sourdough Buns and Rolls

Take your favorite sourdough bread recipe from this book and simply shape them as buns. It's really easy.

Sourdough Buns or Rolls:

Yield: Makes a one loaf batch of dough will make six 4-5 inch buns.

1. Mix the dough and let it ferment in the refrigerator for 24-36 hours as instructed in the recipe.
2. After the cold ferment time, remove from the fridge and let the dough come to room temperature by allowing it to warm on the counter in the bowl for 1 hour.
3. Preheat oven to 450° F (230° C).
4. Then, simply take your measuring cup of choice and scoop out portions of dough onto a cookie sheet lined with parchment paper.
5. When you put the buns in the oven, reduce the heat to 400° F (204° C).
6. Bake for 45-50 minutes turning once at the 30 minute mark to allow for even browning.
7. Cool for 12 hours on a cooling rack or overnight.

13. Recommended Resources

GET ACCESS TO ALL OF THESE RESOURCES WITH CLICKABLE LINKS HERE:

SCAN ME

Recommended Products:

Gluten-Free Flours:
Available at most local health food stores, some major chain grocery stores, Sprouts, Trader Joe's, Whole Foods, Amazon, and online vitamin stores like Azure, SwansonVitamins.com or Vitacost.com. We recommend sourcing organic products!

Arrowroot
Brown Rice Flour
Buckwheat Flour
Flax Meal
Millet
Oat
Potato Starch
Psyllium Husk Powder
Sorghum flour
Tapioca Starch/Flour
Teff
White Rice Flour

Bulk Grains:
Available at Pleasant Hill Grains, local health food stores, some major supermarkets, Azure Standard, Amazon.

Brown Rice
Flax Meal
Millet
Oat
Potato Starch
Psyllium Husk Powder
Quinoa
Sorghum
Tapioca Starch/Flour
Teff
White Rice Flour

THE ART OF GLUTEN-FREE HOMEMADE BREAD

Grain Mills:
Available at Pleasant Hill Grains
Family Grain Mill
KoMo Classic

Baking Equipment:
Available at Pleasant Hill Grains, Amazon, your local cooking store or even thrift stores!

Baguette Pan
Bread Lame or SHARP Knife
Cast Iron Dutch Oven
Cast Iron Dutch Oven with Lid-5 to 6 Quart
Cast Iron Skillet
Cookie Scoop Set
Cuisinart Electric Waffle Maker
Digital Kitchen Scale
Dough Whisk
Doughnut Cutter
Doughnut Pans
French Bread Pan
Loaf Pans- Emile Henry, Covered
Loaf Pans- Glass 1.5 Quart
Loaf Pans- Silicone
Melamine Bowls with Lids
Pastry Brush- Silicone
Pizza Cutter
Reusable Parchment Paper
Rimmed Baking Sheet
Rubber Spatula
Spray Bottle- 4 oz
Thermometer- Quick Read Digital
Waffle Iron- Nordic Cast
Wire Whisks

Further Gluten-Free Reading:

100% Rye by Shannon Stonger

Gluten-Free Artisan Bread in Five Minutes A Day, by Jeff Hertzberg and Zoë François

Gluten-Free Baking for Dummies by Dr. Jean McFadden Layton and Linda Larsen

Promise and Fulfillment by Chris Stafferton

Traditionally Fermented Foods by Shannon Stonger

The Allergy Self-Help Cookbook by Marjorie Hurt Jones

The How Can It Be Gluten-Free Cookbook by America's Test Kitchen

The How Can It Be Gluten-Free Cookbook Vol. 2 by America's Test Kitchen

Wild Bread by Mary Jane Butters

THE ART OF GLUTEN-FREE HOMEMADE BREAD

Index

Agar-agar 23
All-Purpose Baking Mix 19, 28
Almond Flour 9, 28
Amaranth Flour 9, 28
Arrowroot 10, 21, 29, 39, 43, 59, 158
Authentic Foods Classical Gluten-Free Blend 17

Baguette 39, 41, 43, 45, 46, 127, 128, 159
Baking Powder 29, 49
Baking Soda 29, 49
Berries 30
Betty Crocker All-Purpose Gluten-Free Rice Flour Blend 18
Biscuits 28, 29, 32, 33, 35, 36, 42, 47, 50, 96
Black Beans 10
Bob's Red Mill Gluten Free 1-to-1 Baking Flour 18, 22, 28, 79
Bob's Red Mill Gluten-Free All-Purpose Flour 18
Boule 9, 29, 30, 31, 35, 36, 37, 39, 40, 41, 44, 45, 46, 121, 131, 147, 153
Bread 33, 37, 39, 41, 42, 43, 45, 46, 50, 54, 61, 62, 63, 69, 91, 93, 113, 118, 121, 124, 127, 131, 134, 159, 160
Brownies 8, 28, 30, 33, 34, 36, 41, 44, 99, 102, 103, 104
Brown Rice Flour 10, 17, 18, 19, 20, 21, 22, 30, 79, 80, 158
Brown Sugar 31, 105

Buckwheat 10, 11, 30, 31, 39, 41, 43, 46, 58, 64, 131, 158
Butter 31, 51, 06
Buttermilk 32, 41, 46

Cake 77, 85, 89, 99, 101, 102, 108
Cakes 28, 29, 35, 36, 41, 44, 51, 99, 104
Carob Bean Gum 23, 32
Cashew Flour 11, 32
Cassava Flour 11
Celiac 5, 6
Chia Seeds 23, 32, 33
Chickpea Flour 11
Chocolate Chips 33
Cinnamon Rolls 8, 28, 30, 32, 36, 40, 42, 44, 46, 105
Citrus 33, 46
Cocoa Powder 34
Coconut Flour 11, 34
Cookies 28, 30, 31, 32, 33, 34, 35, 36, 38, 44, 47, 51, 94, 95
Corn Flour 11
Cornmeal 12
Cornstarch 12, 19, 34, 39, 43
Crackers 31, 39, 40, 41, 43, 44, 46, 140
Cup4Cup Gluten-Free Flour 19
Cup4Cup Wholesome Flour Blend 19

Doughnuts 28, 30, 32, 36, 39, 40, 41, 42, 43, 44, 46, 105, 108, 110
Dry Climates 115

Eggs 23, 27, 34, 49, 163
Einkorn 5
Equipment 53, 159
Expandex 23

Fava Flour 12
Flatbread 138
Flaxseed 19, 24, 35
Focaccia 138
Frosting 99, 100
Fruit 35, 37

Gelatin 24
Gluten-Free Prairie All-Purpose Baking Mix 19
Glutino Gluten-Free Pantry All-Purpose Flour 20
Guar Gum 21, 24, 35

High Altitude 55, 115
Hodgson Mills Multi-Purpose Baking Mix 20
Honey 35, 37, 42

Icing 92, 106

Khorasan (Kamut) Flour 6
King Arthur Gluten-Free Measure for Measure Flour 20
King Arthur Gluten-Free Multi-Purpose Flour 21

Legumes 12, 64
Lentils 12, 64
Locust Bean Gum 24, 32

Masa Harina 12
Measuring 53
Milk 19, 24, 32, 36
Milk Powder 19, 24, 36
Millet 13, 37, 63
Molasses 37

Monk Fruit 37

Muffins 28, 29, 30, 31, 33, 34, 35, 36, 37, 40, 41, 42, 44, 47, 52, 84, 85, 86, 87, 88, 89, 90

Non-Fat Milk Powder 24

NOW Foods Gluten-Free All-Purpose Flour 21

Nut Butters 38

Nut Flours 13, 64

Oat Flour 13, 19

Oats 13, 38, 58

Oil 38

Pamela's Gluten-Free All-Purpose Flour Mix 21

Pancakes 28, 30, 32, 34, 41, 44, 67, 81, 82

Pectin 24

Pie Crusts 52

Pillsbury Best Multi-Purpose Gluten-Free Flour Blend 22

Pizza 31, 39, 40, 41, 43, 44, 46, 52, 135, 159

Potato Starch 13, 17, 18, 19, 20, 21, 22, 39, 79, 80, 158

Psyllium Husk Powder 24, 39, 158

Quick bread 52, 90, 118

Quinoa Flour 14, 40

Rise Times 55

Rye 6, 160

Salt 18, 40, 50, 115

Scones 28, 29, 32, 33, 35, 36, 42, 47, 53, 96, 97, 98

Soaking 56, 57, 59

Sorghum 14, 18, 19, 20, 21, 30, 37, 38, 40, 58, 63, 79, 80, 104, 158

Sour Cream 41, 46

Sourdough 29, 30, 31, 35, 36, 37, 39, 40, 41, 43, 44, 45, 46, 50, 55, 56, 57, 60, 61, 63, 64, 69, 70, 71, 82, 87, 88, 89, 90, 101, 103, 110, 143, 145, 147, 148, 150, 153, 154, 156

Soy Flour 14

Spelt Flour 6

Spices 42

Sprout 60

Sprouting 56, 58

Starches 64

Stevia 38, 42

Sugar 31, 42, 49, 105, 108, 110

Sweet Rice Flour 15, 18, 21, 42, 79

Tapioca Flour 15, 17, 18, 19, 21, 22, 43

Tapioca starch 13, 15, 23, 28, 110, 118, 121, 124, 127, 131, 135, 137, 138, 140, 145, 147

Teff 15, 43, 59, 158

Tigernut Flour 15

Trader Joe's Baker Josef's Gluten-Free All-Purpose Flour 22

Vanilla Extract 44

Vegetables 44

Waffles 28, 30, 32, 34, 41, 44, 81, 82

Water 36, 44

White Bean Flour 15, 45

White Rice Flour 16, 19, 20, 21, 22, 45, 158

Xanthan Gum 25, 46, 79, 80

Yeast 29, 41, 46, 49, 51, 55, 113, 115, 116, 121, 134

Yogurt 46

Zest 46, 86

About The Authors

Rachel Parks is a Senior Moderator for Homesteading Family. She specializes in bread making, allergy-friendly cooking, and herbal medicine. She is the author of Scoring Sourdough Bread and lives in the NYC area where she homeschools her four children, homesteads from her kitchen, and enjoys teaching homemaking and botany classes. You can follow her at **www.rememberingmaggielane.com**.

Carolyn Thomas and her husband, Josh live on a 40 acre homestead in Idaho surrounded by gardens, livestock and children. She spends her days rocking babies, homeschooling her children and preserving food for the coming winter. As part of her passion she also teaches homesteading skills to encourage other families to live simply and focus on the things that really matter... faith, family and really good food! You can find her at **www.homesteadingfamily.com**.